Don't Call Me Coach

Don't Call Me Coach

A LESSON PLAN FOR LIFE

Phil Martelli

with
HAROLD GULLAN, PH.D.

Foreword by
EDWARD G. RENDELL,
GOVERNOR OF PENNSYLVANIA

CAMINO BOOKS
Philadelphia

Manufactured in the United States of America

1 2 3 4 5 10 09 08 07

LIBRARY OF CONGRESS CATALOGING-IN-PUBLICATION DATA

Martelli, Phil, 1954–
Don't call me coach: a lesson plan for life / by Phil Martelli with
Harold Gullan: foreword by Edward G. Rendell.
p. cm.
ISBN 978-1-933822-06-8 (alk. paper)
1. Martelli, Phil, 1954- 2. Basketball coaches—United States—
Biography. I. Gullan, Harold I., 1931- II. Title.

GV884.M33A3 2007
796.323092—dc22
[B]   2007021747

Interior design: Rachel Reiss

Cover photo by Greg Carroccio/Sideline Photos

This book is available at a special discount on bulk purchases
for promotional, business, and educational use.

PUBLISHER
Camino Books, Inc.
P.O. Box 59026
Philadelphia, PA 19102
www.caminobooks.com

*I would like to dedicate this book to all the "coaches"
in my life who have allowed me to become the person
I am—most especially my parents, Phil and Jane, who
taught me so much with so little fanfare; my wife Judy;
and my children, Philip, Jim, and Elizabeth, who have
sacrificed so I could pursue my dream.*

*I am what I am because I have been touched by the
stars. Each of you is a star.*

Contents

Foreword

I am in my car riding into Philadelphia on a Friday morning listening to 610 WIP, our top-rated all-sports talk radio station. All of a sudden the regular hosts are interrupted by a call from Phil Martelli, the basketball coach of Saint Joseph's University. Phil proceeds to talk Eagles football and then give his predictions for the Sunday game. Now, I'm not sure if Phil Martelli ever played football, and he certainly isn't what you would call an expert, but he was on the radio sounding exactly like any one of the five million Eagles fans in Southeast Pennsylvania.

What a guy! What a true Philadelphian! Phil Martelli is the epitome of a Philadelphian—he is a Rocky Balboa without the muscles and the pompadour. Phil Martelli is one of the most genuine, down-to-earth, and nicest guys you will ever want to meet.

He comes out onto the court for Hawk basketball games looking like he just stepped out of *Gentlemen's Quarterly*. But if you are expecting a cool, Pat Riley type of coach, forget it—because Phil Martelli wears his heart on his sleeve. He is a great coach not only because he is a terrific strategist but because he can inspire kids to believe that nothing is impossible and that there is no dragon they cannot slay. He is also a great coach because he never stops teaching the young men who play for him, whether on the court, in a game, or at practice in viewing them with his incredible basketball sixth sense, or off the court teaching them important life lessons to make them better people.

I will never forget watching Phil on the sidelines in perhaps the two most important games he has ever coached at St. Joe's. The first was the NCAA Round of 16 Tournament game against Wake Forest and the second the heartbreaking loss in the Elite Eight to Oklahoma State and Eddie Sutton. I was sitting in the stands at the Meadowlands with Father Timothy Lannon, the president of the university. The Hawk team was led by two brilliant guards, Jameer Nelson and Delonte West; they were so skilled and so smart it was like having two additional coaches on the court. Phil mapped out a great game plan against Wake Forest, and the Hawks pulled away from the ACC powerhouse. It was tremendous vindication because many sportscasters, including the famous Billy Packer, had said St. Joe's couldn't play with the elite teams in the Atlantic Coast Conference, but as the buzzer sounded I looked at Phil and he was pleased but not too excited because he knew he had to keep his team focused on the next game.

The Oklahoma State game was a nail-biter that went down to the wire with an Oklahoma State player picking up a loose ball and throwing in a three-pointer to put the Cowboys ahead with only seconds to go. The Hawks rushed up the court and a last-second shot to win the game by Jameer Nelson fell just short. As the buzzer sounded, the Hawk players lay dejected on the floor, and my eyes again turned to Phil. After congratulations to Coach Sutton, he immediately went to his team and one by one convinced them that it wasn't the end of the world, that they had given everything they could and that they should be proud of this incredible season.

When I hosted the team and Phil ten days later at the Governor's Residence for a congratulatory dinner there was no dejection or disappointment in their eyes or their voices. Phil had made his case, and there was nothing but pride in what they had accomplished.

St. Joe's is lucky to have this wonderful, charismatic leader, and so is the City of Philadelphia. Phil helps make life fun for all of us—we are consistently amazed and delighted watching him on the sidelines. He cares so much about the city and contributes to helping it in so many ways.

So, just like Rocky, here is hoping that Phil Martelli will always be with us, pacing the sidelines out on City Avenue.

Edward G. Rendell
Governor of Pennsylvania

Acknowledgments

This book wouldn't have been possible without the extraordinary efforts of the engaging Hal Gullan and his patient associate, Elsa Efran; our dynamic Governor Ed Rendell; the loyal Marie Wozniak; the effervescent Clare Ariano; the novice Jack Jumper; the efficient Edward Jutkowitz of Camino Books; the lovely Judy Martelli; our beautiful Elizabeth Martelli; and the many players and dedicated coaches who have allowed me to work with them, creating so many memories over the years. I also want to thank Cathy Rush, Pat Croce, Geno Auriemma, Jim Boeheim, Tom Izzo, Jameer Nelson, and Delonte West for taking the time to share their thoughts with us—and to so many others throughout the Saint Joseph's University community and beyond who have contributed in many ways to this book's success.

Don't Call Me Coach

CHAPTER 1

We Are All Coaches

YES, I REALLY DO TALK TO HAWKS. If not in costume or in the classroom, they're around me all the time, and always on my mind. What they represent, Philadelphia's Saint Joseph's University, is special to me in so many ways. "The Hawk Will Never Die!" has been our rallying cry for as long as I can remember. But, unlike every other college mascot in America, the Hawk also never quits. Somehow the student inside flaps at least one wing, and generally both, throughout every second of every game—something like 3,500 times. Running those figure eights around the court, he (or she) certainly earns a scholarship as much as any player. To me such tenacity not only says a good deal about a person and a school, but a lot about life itself.

I suppose that's why I wanted to write this book. At fifty-three (is that really possible?), I'm not quite ready for an autobiography, but there may be something in my experiences on and off of Hawk Hill, and on and off the court, that will resonate in your life, as well. Anyway, that's what I hope. Wherever you are, whatever you do, this is my conversation with you—life lessons we can share.

Having the title of head coach is very flattering, and when you factor in that there are only 336 jobs like mine—Division I head men's basketball coaches—when you think of how small a portion of the population that represents, you could easily get full of yourself. There's no question that coaching is egotistical. To be successful, I have to believe that I can do it better than the guy at Temple or the guy at Villanova or the guy at St. Bonaventure or the guy at Wyoming. There has to be some ego involved. Still, it's important to take your job more seriously than yourself. It happens that I'm an ordinary person with an extraordinary job. But when we have opportunities, we need to take advantage of them. And, at some point, don't we all have opportunities—and, ordinary or not, don't we all have some talents we can make the most of?

Successful coaching, like success in any other setting, is all about building relationships. It's about being organized, and energizing people. A lot of coaching comes down to maximizing people's skills. And so, when you consider all these things, just about everyone who reads this book is a coach. Everyone who reads it is on a team. If you're part of a family—that's a team; business—that's a team; school—that's a team, as are charities and churches. Whatever you do on a day-to-day basis—you're on a team. And if you're part of a team, then you coach. There's no butcher, there's no baker, there's no candlestick-maker (are they still making candlesticks?) who doesn't build relationships, doesn't organize, energize, maximize the people and the skills and the tools that they have around them. How well do *you* do it?

When I talk to groups, which I do as much as I can, that's my new mantra. To be more successful, why don't you be a more effective coach in your everyday life? But some people don't want that. The more decisive you are, the more open you are to criticism, to second-guessing. And, of course, the more visible you are, the more personal the reaction. I don't relish people sending anonymous letters and e-mails telling me I did something stupid. I don't want someone calling a talk show and saying that I should've called a timeout or should've put in this guy instead of the other guy or should've restrained my reactions to a referee's call. And then there's that latest phenomenon, the message boards, where people simply make up things, and send them out without thinking. We're fortunate in Philadelphia, the most passionate sports city in America, because criticism comes so much more to our professional coaches. By comparison, we college coaches are almost left to ourselves. But you can't be too sensitive and survive in this business.

Whatever your field, you are defined by who you are, not what you do. I've suggested that to be successful in life, you should use more effectively the techniques of coaching that are present in everything. But I don't like being called Coach Martelli, any more than you want to be called Accountant Smith or Salesman Jones or Homemaker Johnson. It's what I do, not who I am. If you will, just call me Phil.

And yet it's true that as a profession, except for some thoughts about law in college, coaching is all I ever wanted to do. I don't recall a time when I wanted to be a fireman or an astronaut or even a pro athlete. Now the fact is that I have a very poor memory. I tell business groups I keep a card in my car with my wife's first name on it, because when I'm preoccupied I don't want to mess things up. It's Judy, by the way. I may resent the fact that she's a better basketball player than I am, but we'll get to that later. Right now I'm trying to remember precisely when this ambition of mine came into my head—coaching the sport, not yet at a specific school. I know that when I was in seventh grade I met a guy named Tom Gallagher who lit a fire under me. He told me that the game of basketball didn't have anything to do with rich or poor, with black or white, with city or suburbs, that it was the ultimate team game, and the ultimate American game. I was already playing it, so it was easy to get hooked.

I believed early on that I had some natural leadership ability. Somehow I could go door-to-door telling kids throughout the neighborhood where and when we were going to get together, and they would show up. Then I could get some guys from other neighborhoods to meet us. So it was natural to play hoops, to have our own pick-up games. It also took fewer players than other sports to make a team. I was always attracted to the game, but as I learned more, I became really interested in the strategies that make it so stimulating. To be honest, at first I thought coaching was all about appearance—suits and walking up and down the sidelines and yelling at referees. The coaches of our Big 5 teams, who I could see on television, became my heroes, larger than life, even more than their players. I didn't have much idea what they really did.

It's odd. Despite having a very poor memory I recall exactly where I was standing, even which way we were facing, when in the eighth grade I said to a friend of mine, Stevie Stefano, "You know, Stevie, some day I'm going to coach the St. Joe's Hawks." Why the Hawks? I can't say to this day. Maybe it was that tireless mascot of theirs, or that their fans were so involved. Maybe it was their coach's demeanor, or that they seemed to win so often. I'd taken the next step. Somehow I knew not only what I wanted to do but where I wanted to do it.

Even at that young an age I realized that I had limitations as a player. Yes, I may be a pretty ordinary guy, but I also thought that, in addition to some leadership ability, I had organizational skills. As the oldest of seven kids at home, sometimes I just had to kind of take charge. Like so many others, my childhood revolved around sports, but from the seventh grade it was all about basketball. By the time I was in the ninth grade, I would go back in the summer and coach fifth graders. I would try to pay back the people who'd helped raise me in the game.

To me, everything about basketball had an allure. Even in its suburbs, Philadelphia is a city of very defined neighborhoods. I lived in Lansdowne in Delaware County, but one of the best places to play was in Yeadon, a predominantly African-American community, at Bell Avenue School. They would play outdoors for hours. I walked one day from Lansdowne to Yeadon to get into a game. It was a tough time in this country racially, and a guy, much bigger than I, stepped up and said, "What are you doing in our neighborhood?" But just then another guy, walking down the street, yelled back to him, "Yo, Phil's a ballplayer. It's OK." It was always OK if you could play, even at my level, just like Tom Gallagher had told me.

In eighth and ninth grade I had a chance to play, although not very successfully, against local legend Joe "Jelly Bean" Bryant, later even better known as Kobe's dad. Older players would take me with them to other popular playgrounds all around the area. Weather willing, basketball's one game you can play indoors or out. But even then I thought of myself more as a coach, a potential organizer. At St. Joseph's Prep, a wonderful school, I started at point guard, and we had a lot of success. By then I realized I hadn't the talent to start for Saint Joseph's University. At Widener University, a Division III program, I played all right, but I would also go out and coach independent teams in my spare time. In my senior year, I like to think I helped to coach my own team as well.

After graduation, going from one high-school coaching and teaching job to another, it often seemed like I paid more in gas than I earned. It would be a twenty-year odyssey before I got to realize my ambition to be the head coach of the Saint Joseph's University Hawks. I was their assistant coach before finally being given the reins in 1995, and it was another nine years before the dream season of 2003–04. I won't deny shedding some tears the day I got the job and the day that season ended, although I try to keep my composure on the court. Of course, this book will focus a good deal on the unforgettable events of that year—the undefeated regular season, being ranked first in the nation, having the consensus most outstanding player in America, and yes, even the consensus Coach of the Year.

As I wrote in the *New York Times* in March 2004, "Saint Joseph's remains the toast of Philadelphia in every church, barbershop, convenience store and talk-radio show. The . . . record speaks for itself, but it pales in comparison with how we have done it . . . so unselfishly, so steadily, in the face of enormous news media exposure and without the showboating and boasting that, sad to say, have become expected." I'm proud of how we played, but prouder of how my players conducted themselves, reflecting so much credit on their university. You don't have to be mega-sized to make a major impact—in academics or athletics.

Of course, we hope to have such success again. The very next year, our overachieving team went to the final game of the National Invitation Tournament. Both seasons ended with an agonizing, last-second shot by the opposing team. It's hard to describe the empty finality of that feeling, when it's all over so suddenly, but you have to try to keep it in perspective. As I said to my players in 2004, "If this is the worst day of your life, then you will have a very blessed life."

Coaching is most of all about teaching and learning, but it can't be done very well without quality players and people. I seem to have become a much better coach after players as talented as Jameer Nelson, Delonte West, and Pat Carroll came into our program. It is not only coaches who demonstrate character. After his final college game, Jameer Nelson, arguably the finest player ever at Saint Joseph's and one of the most admirable people, calmly told the media, "My only goal was to be the best teammate anybody ever had. So because of that, I know we didn't lose today."

For someone so young, he has a remarkable respect for and knowledge of the game. Accompanying Jameer to his ultimate honor, receiving the prestigious John Wooden Award as the outstanding college basketball player in the United States, was just an out-of-body experience. Here I was, sitting next to one of my players and the greatest coach—in my mind the greatest sports manager and leader of all time. And he knows my name, he knows about my team and my players. I was to the point of being speechless because it was John Wooden—in his nineties but just as spry and alert as ever. We met the legendary Pete Newell during that year. We also met Bill Walton. But this was the top. At the presentation it was Jameer who spoke first, then Wooden himself, then me. Someone asked Jameer, "What does this award mean to you?" And he said, "Well, to be sitting here next to the greatest coach of all time..." I couldn't help it. I leaned into my microphone and said, "Aw, thanks, Jameer."

When you reach for a person's hand, you often touch that person's heart. People ask me, "When did you know that team was going to be great? Was it when Jameer told you he was coming back for his senior year?" Everyone knew he had survived the mean streets of Chester, Pennsylvania, and could have made millions by leaving early. My response is no. I first realized I had at least a potentially great team after the preceding season. On March 21, 2003, we'd lost in the first round of the NCAA tournament to Auburn, 65-63 (we seem to make a habit of these final-game squeakers), but had accumulated an impressive 23-7 record overall, 12-4 in the Atlantic 10, and 4-0 in the Big 5.

It was great that Jameer, who'd averaged nearly twenty points a game that season, decided to come back. After his senior season, of course, he still made the NBA and is today a starter for the Orlando Magic. But there had been other questions that needed to be resolved, as well. Although nothing like what happened after the following season, major schools were coming after me. I wasn't going anywhere—you need to know where your heart is—but there can be an awful lot of money in bigtime college coaching, a temptation for anyone. Rumors of conversations with Ohio State and Penn State were floating around, so there was a good deal of uncertainty on Hawk Hill after the 2002–03 season.

It was, however, a very tragic situation, outside of basketball, that really solidified our team for the following year. Dwayne Lee, our fine sophomore guard and defensive stalwart, a product of the outstanding St. Anthony program in Jersey City, had lost his father years earlier. Now his mother was gravely ill. He had gone to visit her around Easter. On his way back, he got a call to get off the train and return home. His mother had taken a turn for the worse. By the time he got there, she had passed away.

We organized the whole team to go up for the funeral. Some of them had never been to a viewing, had never had to deal with losing a loved one. Sometimes we forget how young these kids are. And we took them all up. They all wanted to go. They waited patiently until they could see their teammate alone—the allAmericans, Jameer Nelson and Delonte West; the great shooter from the suburbs, Pat Carroll; players from Philly, from Florida, from Europe, from Maryland and Jersey, black and white, from so many different backgrounds. They each reached for his hand and touched his heart. And that's when I knew this team was going to be special. There was an energy about them, a specialness that transcended mere talent. They had already been a successful team. Now they became a family.

Recruiting is, of course, a very competitive process. I think it helps our recruiting and our program to have a genuinely welcoming attitude, but without being misleading. We don't make promises we can't back up. The young men we recruit, and their parents, can spot a phony very quickly. I hope the experience of every student-athlete who comes to Saint Joseph's will last a full four years, but whatever its duration I want it to be as "real" as the way they were recruited. What I would like our players to think and feel when they leave is that I've dealt with them parentally. And to me parenting is saying "yes" when yes is the appropriate answer, and saying "no" when no is the right response.

I tell everybody we recruit that they will be dealt with fairly. They will not all be dealt with the same. Some guys need a hug, some guys need a kick. Some guys need a shout and some guys need a whisper. If you tell someone that you are going to deal with him the same as the next person and the next person, then you are automatically saying that you are going to deal with him unfairly. From the start I want us to honestly understand each other. The goal is that at the end of the recruiting process or the end of the season or the end of a career, we might have agreed or disagreed on playing time, on accolades, on all of that—but for a player who finishes his career here, I hope he will voice the greatest compliment I can be paid—that he would do it all again. And at the end of the day, I hope he knows I'm still here to help him in any way I can.

When we're in that recruiting process, whether we get the kid or not, I would like his high-school coach and his parents to say, "That was done right." Then I think I've won. Whether the kid turned out to be an all-American or a guy who didn't get off the bench much, if a player will say "I would do it again" and a parent will say the whole process was done right, then I think we've won. And therefore Saint Joseph's University has won. I keep thinking of what Jameer said: "My only goal was to be the best teammate anybody ever had. So because of that, I know we didn't lose today."

Some people say I'm wacky or off the wall. I prefer to think of myself as spontaneous, and believe me, it comes naturally. I can't be any other way. As Sammy Davis Jr. sang, "I've got to be me." When I was asked to host a coach's show on television over a decade ago, I wanted it to be different, to be real, to be believable. This isn't grim world news we're putting out. In an era of really bad television, these shows are in the bottom ten percent. They're really additional revenue streams for the coaches, who are often reluctant to put themselves out there, or to say what they really think. And, honestly, because many of these coaches have pretty bland personalities anyway, their shows are almost unwatchable. So the TV show to me was a unique opportunity. I want that fellow with the remote who finds us to just stop and say, "What the hell is that guy doing?" And then I want him to watch. Because, however crazy it may look and sound, there is always a message.

It may help that, as they say, I have a face for radio and an appearance to match. One writer said I look like an over-the-hill hit man; another, like the guy who comes down each morning to the curb in his pajamas to pick up the newspaper. Our *HawkTalk* is kind of patterned on the old Johnny Carson *Tonight Show,* only without the preparation (or the expense)—taped before a live audience on our campus. My Ed McMahon is the ever-cheerful Joe Lunardi, who works in communications for the university but who now, as ESPN's "bracketologist," is getting more TV exposure than I am. We're largely making it up as we go along. We don't really dwell much on last week's games. That's history.

Oh, we talk sports and we have all kinds of guests, everyone from the governor to the guy who drives our bus—and, of course, everyone involved with the program. But I'm likely to ask them something like, "What's the dumbest thing your coach has ever done?" Still, we get in a lot about the team, pulling no punches, and about the school itself. That, after all, is the idea. Two seasons ago, for example, I said on air, "Let's only have half a show, since we're only really playing about half the time." Once I started the show coming out of a coffin—because our team had been given up for dead. On one occasion I had a "fan" heckle me from behind during the entire program. Once we had a pathetic Saddam Hussein impersonator that Joe and I wound up attacking. Well, you get the idea.

Just about anything can happen, but sponsors like it enough to renew. We seem to have more commercials every season. *The Sporting News*, in fact, called *HawkTalk* the best coach's show in the nation, and now it can be seen nationally. From January to March, it's a ball to do, whatever may have happened the preceding week on the court. And, of course, the input about the university itself is more serious—and positive. Their commercials are a highlight of each show.

Fortunately, my wife can take a joke, and she's been taking mine for the over thirty years we've been married. When I managed to get her to come on the show, against every instinct of common sense she possesses, I gave her a bouquet of not very impressive flowers I pulled out of a battered old shopping bag. It was her fiftieth birthday. She looks so great that didn't seem to faze her. But then later, near the end of the show, I presented her with her "real gift"—a metal walker. Everybody was laughing so hard, there wasn't a dry eye—but hers were rolling, as usual. Still, she comes back once every season.

Maybe it helps that she knows she can still take me one-on-one anytime in the driveway. The former Judy Marra was one of the "Mighty Macs" on the national championship women's teams that Cathy Rush coached at local Immaculata College in the 1970s. Judy and I first met at Cathy's summer basketball camp, where I was working, too. Isn't there a movie called *Love and Basketball*? We certainly didn't steer our three kids in that particular direction, but they've all played, and the two boys are now coaching at colleges, while our youngest, Elizabeth, who played in high school, is a junior at Saint Joseph's.

It may be that the closest I've come to being divorced was not over *HawkTalk* but because of a cell phone and a bathroom. I'm a creature of habit. We used to live eight miles from the campus, just about twelve minutes away. Of course, I liked being so close. I spend a lot of time in my cozy office, reputedly the smallest of any Division I coach in the nation. Its ceiling is so low that some of my players can't even get in without bending over. Now, as I've said, I feel that organization is fundamental to success. I take a lot of notes, but I also rely on my cell phone. My wife thought we should move to a bigger house—which, money aside, was fine with me. She particularly wanted to have a guest bathroom. So we moved out to a home she loves in Media. It's quite a place, a lot more than I'm used to, but it's also at least twenty-five minutes from the campus.

I found to my horror that while driving from the new location in Media to the campus, the cell phone I was using had three dead spots. Maybe it's the hills. Coming in the first day I decided, "I can't deal with this." Driving home was worse. I was about to tell Judy, "Don't unpack the boxes. I can't live this way." But I chickened out. I kind of like being married to her. Instead, I went out and bought a Dictaphone. So now when the service goes out on the way to City Line Avenue, I talk to myself on that and later play it back. And Judy has her bathroom, or half-bath, whatever it's called, that only visitors are permitted to use. I call it our visiting team's locker room, but it's a lot nicer than the one at Alumni Memorial Fieldhouse.

Speaking of making use of earlier technologies, this past year I was talking to a group of students about leadership, how it relates to coaching and life. I made a non-Power Point presentation that included the story about the Dictaphone. After I left,

Don DiJulia, our athletic director, remained to answer questions. A young woman raised her hand and asked, "Coach talked about Dictaphone. Was that a combination iPod BlackBerry?" Back to the future.

Efficiency never goes out of style. When people start to look at their own communicating skills and how to build relationships, whether they plan to be coaches or not, organization is critical. It may sound boring, but I find the process of organizing to be a joy. I love logistics. If I've been at all successful it's because of the quality of people I've been surrounded with, and how we work as a team, not just X's and O's on the court, but laying things out beforehand and seeing how they fit.

But, as noted, there's also a place for spontaneity, for an environment of excitement. I like to have a kind of swirl, not just around me, but around everything I'm doing. I can't wait to dive into the daily pile of mail. As opposed to a lot of coaches, I love summer basketball camps—because you never know what's going to happen. You meet some of these kids—they are so excited to be there. I want to give them more than just my time of day. I want to give them a high-five or a pat on the back. I want our camp to have a personality and a pizzazz that makes it different from other camps.

When it comes to public speaking, I never want mine to sound like coach-speak. I don't want it to be from a script. I want it to be from my head and my heart. Yet in order to do this, to efficiently do anything—to efficiently be a husband, or efficiently be a father, or efficiently be a coach, I know that I have to have my columns in order. You can talk spontaneously, but it helps to think about it first. Speaking's fine, but sometimes when I give interviews, or when I react to the comments of others, that's when I can get in trouble, when I just talk off the top of my head. But, honestly, it's almost always because I feel someone has slighted my school or my team or both. It's never personal. These thankfully few instances, too, will be in this book—with Lute Olson, Billy Packer, and that painful incident with an old friend, John Chaney, where I did manage to show restraint. Then, of course, there are those last-minute calls by referees.

Some people may feel that even my spontaneity is practiced, but that's not true. I don't consciously say, "I'm going to do it this way because Mike Krzyzewski does it that way, or Geno Auriemma, or Jim Calhoun." I don't consciously pattern my style after anyone, or in contrast to anyone. In fact, there is no actual "style" at all. What you're seeing is Phil Martelli. You might want to see Coach Martelli, but I prefer that you see Phil Martelli, flaws and all. I know there are flaws and I know there are idiosyncrasies, but so long as there's nothing calculated, I can live with them. And coaching always comes first.

We have only one team rule, and that is to be on time, the ultimate sign of respect. I tell my players: I'm not here to spend your money, but my job is based on investing your time. Now I admit I push the envelope for myself because I've actually timed the red lights all the way from Media. Unless it's an illness or a class I know about, there's no reason for a player to be late for practice. Being organized, I do use my cell phone a lot. There are no dead spots in my bedroom. I call the office in the middle of the night and leave myself a voice-mail full of reminders. So as soon as I arrive I can get started at once. I don't have to wait for the action to develop. All of our team practices are open to the public. If we're prepared, we've nothing to hide, and it helps to get the feel and absorb the noise of even a small crowd during practice.

Our home court may hold only 3,200 people, but with that drum going and the fans in a frenzy, it can sound like 32,000. In 2003, *Sports Illustrated* included high in a list of "The 100 Things You Have to Do Before You Graduate" going to a Saint Joseph's basketball game and yelling "'The Hawk Will Never Die' . . . the most defiant cheer in college sports."

We've also had a far larger home away from home over the years, Penn's storied Palestra, the most historic arena in college basketball. During the decades St. Joe's has played there we've won nearly seventy percent of the time. The 2005–06 season marked the fiftieth anniversary of Philadelphia's unique Big 5, with most of its memorable games played at the Palestra. Including Drexel, with six Division I basketball schools within seventeen miles of each other, there's no rivalry remotely like it anywhere else in the nation.

Although our "holy war" with Villanova, Jesuits vs. Augustinians, may be our most anticipated rivalry each season, our games against Penn, Temple, La Salle, and Drexel are just as contentious. The overall Atlantic 10 schedule does the most to determine our postseason plans, but every game is pivotal. We had no more dramatic contest in 2006 than our hard-fought victory over Penn in the Big 5 official fiftieth anniversary game at the Palestra, with nostalgic streamers coming down to the court—just like in the old days.

That, too, is part of the Saint Joseph's story—and, along with cheesesteaks and history, what makes Philadelphia such a tough place ever to leave. The legendary Big 5 coaches, from Temple's Harry Litwack, 'Nova's Jack Kraft, La Salle's Tom Gola, Penn's Chuck Daly, and our own Dr. Jack Ramsay, were as competitive as any in America, but they also personified civility and cooperation before and after every game. They dined together every week. Their players were like brothers who fight ferociously among themselves, but heaven help an outsider who takes on any one of them. To this day, when we're not playing against each other, we pull for each other's teams and join together in such major charitable causes as Coaches vs. Cancer, to use whatever clout we have to give back to others. I'll tell you more about it.

But first, let's go back to where my own dreams began, took shape, and led me to this place: the Martelli family—from Mount Clemens, Michigan, to Southwest Philly to suburban Lansdowne to Clifton Heights to Norristown to Drexel Hill to Media, but most of all to Hawk Hill.

CHAPTER 2

The First Team Is Family

YOU DON'T HAVE TO BE FROM PHILLY TO BE A "PHILLY GUY." I was born in Michigan and live in the suburbs, but I bleed Eagles green as well as St. Joe's crimson and gray. I cheer on our "blue collar" athletes, whatever their team, more for their effort than their style. If they're underdogs, all the better. It's hard to define, but to me being a Philly guy means overcoming obstacles, giving something back, having a passion for life—not just sports, but going at it with just a bit of an edge, and the kind of ironic, often self-deprecating humor that comes from experience. But perhaps most of all, being up-front with everybody, not letting down the people who believed in you. As my friend Geno Auriemma said when he was inducted into the Naismith Memorial Basketball Hall of Fame, "All I ever wanted was the respect of how I do things and how I represented my family, my school, my program. And this is the ultimate sign of respect."

So being a Philly guy isn't really limited by geography. Plain talk can come from a Missouri president, a Wyoming cowboy, a "Southie" from Boston, a south-sider from Chicago, a surfer from L.A.—or even a "Jersey guy" like Bill Parcells. Nor is it limited by race or religion. When my Jewish friends refer to a "mensch," I think they're really describing what it means to be a standup Philly guy. Someone you can count on. And as for gender, my perceptive, athletic, straightforward, but unpretentious wife may be the quintessential "Philly girl."

Still, I love Philadelphia and everything it represents, starting with its history, which is really the birthright of all Americans, wherever they live and wherever their families came from. But most of all because my own family has grown up—and continues to live—around here. Please keep those cards, letters, and job offers coming. They do a lot for my ego. But let me be honest, the first requisite of being a Philly guy. It would be hard to leave.

Wherever *you* may find yourself living today—and ours is certainly a mobile society—your first team was and is your own family. Your first coaches were your parents, and their first gift to you the family name you share. It seems to me, whether your earliest memories were of the kind of modest row house I grew up in or something a good deal more palatial, whether you were blessed with two parents or a devoted single parent or grandparent, they are still the source of whatever you may have become. Everything else, hopefully positive, is reinforcement. As you grow over the years from being a member of that first team to mentoring your own, even as everything else may have changed, that family name remains. It's yours to respect, protect, sustain, and pass on—whatever you wind up doing with your own life, and no matter how much the indifferent winds of change and chance may have diminished your own dreams.

That's a message I deliver a lot in recruiting. That when you come to Saint Joseph's University, you represent first and foremost yourself. Second of all, your family. And third, you're going to represent me because there's a stamp on your head saying I brought you here. It isn't all that different in the corporate world. Somebody, a headhunter or human resources person, selected you to work there. So everything you do, and every way you do it, reflects on the person who put you in that position. Tell me a job that doesn't require your respecting your own name, the family name you've inherited, and the name of the person who hired you—or, in our case, the coach who recruited you. Life may not always be fair, but *you* should try to be.

No disrespect to you welcome readers from the great state of Michigan, but I happen to have been born there because my father was in the Air Force. The date was August 31, 1954. The location—the hospital on the grounds of Selfridge Air Base. My parents, married for only a year, lived in a snug, first-floor apartment some ten to fifteen minutes away in Mount Clemens. They had so little money to gas up my father's proudest possession, his first car, that it was often a question of whether he'd get to the base before running out. I don't imagine he could just glide down from Mount Clemens, whatever its height.

My mother went into labor on August 30. Just after midnight my father, a skilled radio operator who had to be on duty that morning, managed to get her to the base hospital. It may be hard to believe, in view of my placid demeanor today, but apparently I was a most difficult delivery. It was some twelve harrowing hours before Dad received the message he'd hoped for. I'd finally arrived. An apparently healthy boy, just under seven pounds, a "beautiful, tow-headed" blond. Naturally. A second message followed shortly thereafter, this one directly from my mother, "Hon, they want to know his name."

Now my father is Philip Edgar Martelli. My grandfather was, of course, Edgar Philip Martelli, although they rarely used their middle names. I became simply Philip Martelli. My gentle but strong-willed mother, Mary Jane McCormick Martelli, just didn't like the idea of a "junior." Maybe she thought I'd find it inhibiting, or bigger kids would beat me up. Of course, friends of my father thought of me as Jr. anyway, just as with the George Bushes. And, like me, my father prefers simply to be called "Phil." Whatever, I carry the two names that mean the most to me.

It might make for a more colorful account if we could chronicle the volatile melting-pot saga of an American family headed by an Italian-American father and an Irish-American mother, like a TV sitcom. But my parents were and are anything but volatile, except perhaps at basketball games, and we've never really thought in those terms. Again, no disrespect to anyone's heritage; it's something to be cherished, but our antecedents are rather far removed from that past. We're just a typical American family with a lot of interesting relatives. My great-grandfather Martelli, indeed, was born somewhere in Italy, but we're not quite sure where. An uncle's laborious attempt at a family tree just kind of vanished. It's too bad. Apparently the Martellis have as many branches as Wachovia Bank. My father thinks we have relatives in France. He was born on, naturally, the south side of Chicago, although he grew up in Philadelphia. My mother's grandparents emigrated from Ireland, and settled in South Philly to stay.

It may get easier to keep track of things in the future. My grandfather Martelli came from a family of ten children. My parents had seven. An eighth, another son, died tragically after just a few days. My wife, Judy, and I have only three offspring—finally an official Philip Jr., Jimmy, and Elizabeth. As noted, although motivated just as we were by our parents to find their own path in life, the boys have chosen to perpetuate the family business and are both coaching college basketball. One had been on my team at Saint Joseph's. The other played at Dickinson College. Our daughter, a three-sport athlete in high school, is starting her junior year at Saint Joseph's. She had been at Boston College, a wonderful school, but just couldn't stay away.

I was fortunate enough growing up to have Grandfather Martelli very much around. Were I writing this for the *Reader's Digest*, he would undoubtedly be the "most unforgettable character" I've known. He'd also demolish any ethnic stereotypes you may still harbor. Edgar Philip Martelli was a very private person who never said much, but he must have been driven to work really hard at jobs he rarely mentioned. He lived in South Philadelphia and was loyal to the traditions of that neighborhood, but he was hardly your stereotypical "Italian." There were no immense Sunday meals at two in his home, no Blessed Mother statue in his window, no careful coverings to protect his sofa, and very little hugging, even of his favorite grandson. He was decidedly *not* warm and fuzzy. His wife had died before I was born, and he lived for many years with a very nice lady who we called simply "Anna." To my knowledge they were never married. Whether common-law wife or live-in girlfriend, this wasn't exactly the social or religious norm at that time and place. However, it seemed perfectly natural to them. They were happy, and that was all that mattered.

What I most remember is that, whatever you wanted, Grandfather Martelli always had "a guy." You know the vernacular: "I know a guy." We never went through the front door of a store. We'd meet in an alley, and wind up on the third floor. My grandfather just always knew somebody on the inside. As the saying goes, "I can get it for you wholesale." He must have had a lot of contacts.

When I was about to get engaged, a college senior with no money, Judy asked tactfully about a ring. That's one little detail I hadn't quite worked out. Not knowing what to do, of course I went to see my grandfather (no, I didn't kiss his ring). With little fanfare he simply went down into the basement and emerged with a stack of fresh one-hundred-dollar bills. Was he printing them down there? Then he directed me to go to "Jewelers' Row" down on Sansom Street, where he "had a guy" I should see. I tapped on his window three times (honestly), and the guy let me in. "You must be Oscar's grandson," he said. (At the time, my grandfather worked for Oscar Mayer.) He already knew what I wanted. What a beautiful ring. It remains a kind of bond between the generations of our family.

My grandfather lived long enough to see me have some success in coaching, but he never asked for a dime in return for the ring. He had also bought me my first car. I didn't know a thing about cars, and still don't, beyond the fact that they have an ignition and run on gas. I didn't even get a driver's license until I was twenty. I just couldn't be bothered. In those innocent days I was just as happy to hitchhike everywhere. Well, I was driving back from somewhere, preoccupied as usual, and the car simply broke down in the middle of a very busy intersection. Not knowing what to do, I did the obvious—I called my grandfather. He came and got the car, and it simply disappeared. He never mentioned it again, nor did I.

Beyond working—and either it must have been pretty profitable or he was a really successful saver—Grandfather Martelli's other great passion was photography. He had one of those really big cameras and videotaped everything, giving us an enormous library of VCR tapes. I guess you'd say he was just ahead of his time. Looking back, I wish we had talked more. He must have had some fascinating stories to tell.

We may not all have a grandfather as unique and generous as mine, but we all have family connections (not just knowing a guy downtown) that are worth cherishing. I don't remember my mother's father quite so well because he died when I was young. I do recall Grandfather McCormick taking me downtown on the trolley one Christmas to see a movie, and that Grandmother McCormick, although sick with diabetes, was always the life of the party. Yes, there was some drinking on that side of the family, and yes, their origins were good-hearted Irish.

I do see something of Grandfather Martelli in my father, although he's a lot more talkative, and unfortunately there wasn't room in our basement to print money. My father is probably the hardest–working person I've ever seen, although you'd never know it to talk to him. He'd rather talk about *us*. Affection comes in many forms. There wasn't a lot of hugging in our home either, but growing up none of us ever doubted how deeply our parents loved us. Most of all, we were encouraged to learn, and then reach for whatever it was we dreamed of. Only our means were limited, never our goals—or our sense of security as a family.

I can understand why my parents, now both in their seventies, have had lifelong friends they retain to this day, all the way from childhood. I don't have many friendships like that. Perhaps a career in coaching discourages it. I've been blessed with some great friends, but most of them are more recent. Even with those from seventh or eighth grade, it's not monthly dinners or regular parties at people's homes or the kind of special occasions my parents have enjoyed. In fact, it was my father's teenage buddies who, in effect, led him to Michigan, and to my being born there.

I may be the first Martelli, at least from our branch of the family, to graduate from college, but I wasn't the first to start. My dad, a good student and athlete at John Bartram High, had completed his freshman year at a local extension campus of Penn State University before he decided to enter the service. Money was tight and the Korean War still raging when he and six or seven of his friends, hanging out in South Philly, decided on the spur of the moment to join up together. There they were, just "standing on the corner, watching all the girls go by," when they made that decision. Of course, by then this Phil Martelli had only one girl in mind. He was already a man.

Four years later, married and a father, discharged and back home, he understood that there was no realistic possibility of his going back to college. Our growing family came first, as it always would. My parents simply accepted their responsibilities, even embraced them. Each of us, the seven very different children they raised, feel fortunate today to still have both our parents so much a part of our lives, our children's, and their children's. Our first coaches, they led by example. What they didn't say was as important as what they did. They never voiced regret about opportunities they had missed in their own lives, only encouragement for each of us to follow our own dreams, which became theirs. Whatever the pressures they faced, I never recall them raising their voices or arguing with each other. And I don't recall a word of bigotry directed toward anyone, a solid foundation for the profession I chose to pursue. My parents gave respect to everyone they met. That's what jumps out at me today, all the way from grade school—my parents are respectful people.

I don't want to make them seem unique or heroic or larger than life. It wasn't quite the Waltons or Norman Rockwell in our home (you *do* remember them?), smiles all the time. The fact is, as you'll see, demonstrative or not, my parents are both characters. It seems to run in our family. But there *was* a kind of quiet heroism in how they raised us. You don't need to be hugged and kissed all the time to know you are loved. When I went off to college, already a Philly guy who wears his emotions on his sleeve, and vowed to make my parents proud of me, we may have even shared a few tears.

My earliest clear memories are of living in a row house on Shield Street in Southwest Philly. There were only three bedrooms, maybe more like two and a half, and we lived there until I was twelve, at the time the oldest of six children. Without realizing it, as additional siblings came along, I learned what it meant to be the oldest, to help set an example. We had more bunk beds than a submarine. To mix the services, I must have been something like a first sergeant. My father tells me, however, that I was more like Red Skelton (you *do* remember Red Skelton?), my imitations cracking everyone up. I'd throw quarters (where did they come from?) into the unused fireplace, yell "scramble," and watch the other kids go after them. Nothing malicious, of course, just the life of the party. Maybe we should try that on *HawkTalk*, although no guest is likely to out-scramble Joe Lunardi.

Did we have a fireplace then? It may have been later. Like most people, my memories of childhood are less distinct than all mixed together. What emerges is an amalgam of vivid impressions of *how* as much as *where* we lived. We weren't really poor, or at least we didn't think of ourselves as poor. We always had every essential we needed, within reason. (Of course, I later discovered my grandfather's largesse.) But if that was so, it's because my father worked so hard. I have a clear recollection of him going out each morning, coming back for dinner, and then going to a second job in the evening.

For over forty years, Dad worked in the research laboratories at DuPont. His evening job was at Misericordia Hospital in West Philadelphia. He would meticulously prepare that day's billing so that each patient could settle up before leaving the following morning. I suppose, under other circumstances, that he might have become an esteemed scientist or an affluent accountant. Instead he was just a great dad. And a good man. How often I've heard people say, to this day, "Your father is a really good man." That just about defines him.

If hard work was a fact of life, so was the importance of education. We were encouraged not just to do well in school but to become well-rounded, which also meant well-read. To this day I'm a ferocious reader, but it all began with Chip Hilton, the Hardy Boys—and my mother. She was a traditional "stay-at-home mom," which simply seemed natural to us. It would be considered some sort of rare aberration today. She may not have gone to college, but it hardly inhibited her education. She loved to read, and shared that love with each of us, starting with me. We'd go to the library together, each with our own card. Most of what we children learned within the emotional security of our household wasn't so much imposed as absorbed. Reading with my mother opened new vistas for me. If seeing is believing, she helped me to see.

My mother didn't go to work, at least in terms of outside the home, until about the time I was in the eighth grade, and we had moved to the suburbs. She became a waitress at a hotel restaurant near the University of Pennsylvania. Some extra income was probably necessary, but it must have been a difficult transition for her. As usual, we heard no complaints. As I recall, she worked from about 6:30 in the morning to three, and so was still there when we returned from school each day. In the truest sense, both my parents have always been there for us.

A lot of my earliest education, little viewed that way at the time, was on the playgrounds, open lots, and streets of Southwest Philly. I don't recall a time I didn't love sports. They weren't quite so organized in those days, but fortunately there were a lot of good adults around to help us go in the right direction. Even when there weren't, it was perfectly safe for us kids on our own to go out and play spontaneously almost anywhere throughout our neighborhood. Was that a hundred years ago?

I was a "city rat," playing football, basketball, and baseball, each in its own season, and I loved them all. Only later did I get that epiphany about the unique qualities of basketball, and my destiny on Hawk Hill. Perhaps trying to lead my siblings helped, but wherever that ability may have come from, somehow I was able to organize kids on the playgrounds, get them to work together, help set up our games, and even start thinking about strategy. That instinct was evident to me early on. We *all* have abilities. As I began to discover the creativity that playing each game entailed, I suppose I became a kind of coach, but playing was still my passion.

I do clearly remember Finnegan Playground. It was kind of our home base. When I was eight or so, sports had become the center of my little universe. But honesty impels me to relate that I was also an honor student at school, with perfect attendance. I loved school, just about every subject, much to the relief of my parents. I was also an altar boy. Like everything else, my parents' staunch Catholic faith was and is understated, but it has always been there—a significant part of our heritage. We went to Mass at St. Barnabas Church as a family every Sunday. I don't mind being characterized today as having a "faith-based philosophy" of coaching and teaching, so long as it's clear that the faith I profess doesn't exclude those of other faiths. I still feel we're all here for a higher purpose that we'll discover in time.

When I was in seventh grade the little row house we had long outgrown was finally left behind. We set out for the pleasant town of Lansdowne, in the near-western suburbs of Philadelphia. Our neat new home, on its own modest lot, was hardly imposing, but it looked like a palace to us—perhaps twice the size of our old place. Forty years later, my parents still live there, although it's frequently also inhabited by the children of their children's children, and their equally active canine companions. There may even be a bit more hugging now, but the affection is almost certainly as evident as it was when we were growing up.

My parents are not all that similar in personality. My mother is rather reserved, almost nervous at times, especially when rival teams' fans may be hurling abuse at her oldest son, and she's not particularly fond of crowds. My father may not be demonstrative, except in terms of questioning the calls of vision-impaired officials, but he is incredibly garrulous, and he loves crowds. What is more important, and I think is the secret of a good marriage and good parenting, is that both of my parents have always viewed what really matters in life in pretty much the same way.

The funny thing is that in our family Dad is kind of the butt of most of our jokes. My wife, Judy, who wasn't raised in quite the way we were, thinks this can be disrespectful, but it's really more a matter of fondness. You know, every family has a sort of secret set of stories, an internal dynamic that isn't easily shared with even those we marry.

My father can be a kind of absent-minded professor, sort of like Columbo on TV (you must remember him). There are times when he seems to be talking largely to himself. But he's also talking with everyone else, so he's always gathering information. The fact is, he's really sharp. He knows everything that's going on, but he can seem so muddled he'll want to keep talking with you about seven new subjects after you've made your point and departed. When you drive with him you know he's going to get lost, and the one conversation he won't have is to ask for directions. He may suddenly remember that he had to go to the drugstore. Maybe that was an hour ago, and you're all about to leave—but no, it has to be done right now. I have twin nieces who are four years old, and when you tell them, "You're going to ride with Pop," they roll their eyes and respond, "Oh, no!" Yet they love him no less than we do.

They and the rest of our family comprise one of my dad's two greatest interests now. The other is St. Joe's basketball. He's really into the message boards, ESPN, and all the rest. He tracks down all the rumors, who's recruiting whom, with his customary thoroughness. He rarely gives me advice on what to do. It's not in his nature to be intrusive, to ask about playing time or strategy. Yet, if you go up in the stands with him, he knows absolutely everything that's going on, and he'll tell you who should start. He's also the eternal optimist. It always looks to be the best team he's ever seen, with the best young players—and, of course, the best coach.

Once I really got into basketball, I don't think my father, no matter how many hours he'd worked or how tired he was, ever missed a game I played in. So that started a long time ago.

Growing up, I was the only one of his children really into team sports. Although he didn't drag all the others to every game, there must have been times when they thought he was crazy. "Why is he always watching Phil?" And maybe there was even a little bit of sibling jealousy. But he kept coming, and my mother too, made most of them—especially when I was in high school and college. They both come today.

Now that he's retired, I can count on my father being at every St. Joe's practice, as well as every game—home or away. My mother, not so much the optimist, isn't that fond of some of the away games. As noted, she doesn't always like the language she hears, and she's no better a loser than I am. Only she prays. I no longer cry, as I did as a boy, over losses, at least not most of the time, but I still simmer.

You'll have to bear with me if I seem to be preaching. I keep thinking about how I was raised, my relationships within my own family, and how it may relate to yours. Throughout our society I believe kids need to be loved, something beyond being befriended. My parents didn't exactly befriend me, but there was never any doubt that they loved me. I hope my affection for my own children and my extended family, my players, is evident—but I'm not their buddy. As cited in the first chapter, I try to act parentally. Sometimes that means saying no. I'm sure you don't want to read about what makes us Martellis so special. The fact is, we're not special, just as typically varied as your own family probably is. But perhaps you might find some relevance in considering how differently we all turned out, the seven children who grew up on Clearbrook Avenue in Lansdowne, Delaware County, Pennsylvania.

My sister Marianne, the oldest girl, is an athlete. She runs marathons, and she's a fitness instructor. She works for a law firm but she's very, very physically fit, in far better shape than I ever was.

My sister Rosemarie is a critical-care nurse for infants. She's married to a basketball coach, and her son coaches college basketball. She's a great fan and student of the game. All my sisters have been supportive, but particularly Rose.

Now my sister Patti Anne really feels this book should be about her. She's much funnier than I am, and perpetually puzzled about why I seem to get so much publicity. Moreover, in addition to being a mother, she has a unique job as administrative assistant for a very rich man. I'd better find a way to bring her into this later.

My sister Christine is the family eccentric (perhaps I should say the *most* eccentric). She's wild. Like Sybil, she is so fast and frenzied in living her life that waves are created in her wake. She works at WaWa now, but is also back in school working for her degree at Immaculata.

My only brother Stephen is a certifiable genius, with the IQ to prove it. Unfortunately, it got him separated from the University of Chicago after a little disagreement with a professor about grades. In effect, Stephen insisted, "I'm here to gain knowledge, not grades. They're only your opinion of what I've learned. I'm the best judge of that." It turned out that the professor disagreed. Stephen never went back to college, got immersed in the culinary arts, and at least for a time became a skilled chef. Once he gets into it, he can become an expert at almost anything. Now it's sports. Unlike my father, he calls me constantly about basketball strategy. Of course, he's learned a lot, but boy, he does run on. My only sibling who's out of the area, Stephen lives in Chicago now. If we could widen our conversational possibilities a little, I'd love to see him more.

I'm embarrassed to relate that I'm not quite certain how old everyone is. I'm pretty sure Stephen is in his forties. As I've said, affection can come in many forms. In our family you're not likely to get cards for birthdays or anniversaries, but as the saying goes, it's the thought that counts. I was to have had a second brother,

Michael, but he died after only a few days. It was a rare blood disease that was known as "blue baby" syndrome. I'm certain my parents took it hard, but even their grief was internalized.

My youngest sister, Lisa, was born when I was fifteen. I'm proud to be her godfather, but because I married at twenty-one, I didn't really get to know her growing up as well as I did the others. Lisa's a good illustration of how wrong it can be to label people, especially when they're young. She was very quiet, by choice, but probably also inhibited because her four older sisters weren't hesitant in telling her what to do.

For the first six years of school, Lisa was labeled a "special ed" child because she was so quiet. In those days they didn't really test and didn't really know. When, in seventh grade, she transferred from public to Catholic school, and went on to Archbishop Prendergast High, she improved academically—straight A's all the way. The silent can also be smart. And, of course, Lisa became a lot less silent. She enrolled at Cabrini College, where she really blossomed. Now pursuing her Ph.D. in reading, she is also a great teacher at a public school.

I'm as proud of all my siblings as I hope they are of me, even though I don't always remember specific dates, as I should. You too may think you're ordinary, but we all have special gifts. We just need people around us who care enough to keep prodding to help those gifts emerge. Yes, I was a good student, but not a top performer. I was always a good athlete, but not the best. My sister Marianne is a better athlete, especially now. My brother Stephen is smarter. My sister Christine is more creative. My sister Rosemarie saves lives. My sister Lisa has more grit. And my sister Patti Anne is much funnier than I am. She'll tell you that herself.

There are little kids of seven or eight who do wonders with music, with mechanics, especially with computers—far beyond my comprehension. The potential gifts I had—to lead and to organize, the eventual makings of a coach—had to be uncovered by people with the eyes to see and the interest to care. My parents had encouraged me to follow my own path. Now as the placid 1950s vanished into the volatile 1960s, they were especially happy that I had found the positive structure of sports. I would be secure as part of a group of guys doing the right things, guided by responsible adult mentors they could trust. It was up to me to take advantage of such opportunities.

In that sense, moving to the suburbs when I was twelve really focused my life. I still loved other sports, but I was bitten by the basketball bug. As great as it had been to play on our own, everything was so much more organized. There was so much to learn. I met up with the CYO coaches at St. Philomena Parish— Peter O'Keefe, Tom Gallagher, and John Steel—who introduced me to the inner workings of basketball. I remember thinking, "Man, this is a great game." It was also a good way to be accepted in a new neighborhood. If you had some potential talent, it didn't matter if you were big or small. You didn't have to be the fastest or the tallest. Everybody could have a role in this game. I learned early that mine would be as a point guard, the distributor of the ball. I could understand the concepts that people like Tom Gallagher were imparting to me, a revelation of the game's complexity. It tore me up when Tom died so young in 1997. I tried to be selfless on the court, but I liked the feeling that I had the game in my hands, and didn't mind telling people about it. Unfortunately, that could lead to an occasional crack on the mouth by an older kid who resented it.

As a veteran of the tough city game, I knew that, whatever my shortcomings, I was already better than most of these suburban kids. Having made the transition from my old school and neighborhood may help to explain why, unlike my parents, I haven't retained all those intimate friendships from childhood. For a time my old gang from Southwest Philly would find their way out to play. I wanted to be on the court every day. But inevitably that began to fade away as I made new friends and teammates in seventh and eighth grade. Many of those I've retained, but going off to high school at St. Joseph's Prep back in Philly, which still draws students from throughout the area, led to a whole new set of acquaintances.

It is embarrassing to recount, since (despite an occasional lapse) I try to stress self-control today, what a mouthy, brash braggart I could be when we first got to Lansdowne. Thinking that at least comparatively I was pretty good, I just ran my mouth, forgetting everything my parents had imparted. Maybe it was insecurity, but it ended when some of the older kids, whose games I wanted to get in on, simply dumped me head-first into a trash can—an apt antidote for trash-talking. But the fact is, they could also see some potential, once I shut up and let my game do the talking.

I was fortunate that so many kids my age really enjoyed basketball. It had become as popular in the spreading suburbs that surrounded Philly as in the city itself, with emerging rivalries—parochial, public, and private—throughout the region. So when I would spread the word, "Let's meet at three o'clock," I knew that there would be ten or twelve who were ready to play. And those older guys in my new neighborhood, who eventually took me under their wing, would take me along to games in other neighborhoods. They knew, mouth and all, that even when I was in eighth grade, I could play a bit on their level. That's what was so intriguing to me about the game, and helps account for its universality today. You could go from place to place, neighborhood to neighborhood, and it was always the same game. But when you got there you had to prove yourself all over again. "It's OK. He's a player," that black kid had told his friend when I ventured into their neighborhood during the strife-torn sixties.

I was surely no paragon, but I wasn't raised to see color. Certainly, most of my classmates were white, but we had one black kid at St. Philomena's who was clearly a better all-around basketball player than any of the rest of us, and a good guy as well. I didn't mind being second to him. His name was Gene Carey, and he's coaching today in an independent league. Our most outstanding player at the Prep was Mo Howard. What I hated was losing, losing to anyone. I was an awfully sore loser. It would crush me to lose. Some say there is "no crying in baseball" (I guess they never saw the Little League World Series), but when my basketball team lost, particularly my grade-school team, there was crying in the Martelli household. I never got that emotional about football or baseball or any other sports.

I played football because it was the social thing to do, like the "flavor of the month" back in Philly. Naturally, I was a quarterback, with the ball in my hands, which hopefully might attract more girls. The hormones were just beginning to kick in. Unfortunately, I was not only slow of foot, but not crazy about getting hit. I simply had no interest in learning the strategy of the game, and gave it up after eighth grade. But I studied basketball. Yes, I'm proud I was a good student, but it's almost like I majored in basketball at a very young age.

And then in eighth grade I announced to a bemused Stevie Stefano that one day I would be the head men's basketball coach at Saint Joseph's University, up on the hill that divided Philly from Montgomery County, only a few miles from where we were standing. The Big 5, the most remarkable college basketball structure in the nation, was in its heyday. With the addition of Drexel, here were six major Division I basketball schools within a single region—Villanova out on the Main Line, but the others all within the city of Philadelphia: Saint Joseph's, La Salle, Temple, and the host school in its mythical Palestra, the University of Pennsylvania—playing each other and just about every other major basketball power in televised nighttime doubleheaders every winter weekend. Nothing else quite like it.

Why would anyone immersed in the best college basketball competition want to leave Philly? Every family had its own favorite, whether any family member had gone to that school or not. You had to have a team to root for. My adopted school was St. Joe's. My father insists to this day that it originated with him, a loyalty that became mine by inheritance.

Well, it's possible. I remember back in Southwest Philly, the old neighborhood, we used to take the 36 trolley to the Palestra in West Philly, by the Penn campus. I couldn't have been more than ten. Somehow we found the money to go to those double-headers almost every Friday and Saturday night, and adults to take us. As challenging as it is to define what makes a "Philly guy," I'm really not sure what hit me first about St. Joe's. I'd kind of laid out the litany to Stevie, but in person it was so much more compelling. Imagine a coach so courtly they always called him *Dr.* Jack Ramsay, down on one knee, calmly surveying the field of battle like General Patton, but then suddenly getting right into it. That unique Hawk mascot, running those figure eights around the court, wings flapping until the seconds ran out. The loudest drum in America, and the loudest fans, shouting the most defiant war cry since Geronimo's, "The Hawk Will Never Die!" I suppose that's all a part of it. And St. Joe's was very, very good in those days. But today I will tell you that most of all it was the passion. I didn't know how to put it then.

You can't measure it, but you can feel it, even when games are played in the Alumni Memorial Fieldhouse on Hawk Hill, with only a third of the capacity of the old Palestra. It's more than noise. The passion is always there, the expectations always high. I mean no disrespect to those other fine schools in the Big 5, but it just seemed to me, a kid in grade school, that someday I'd wind up as the coach of St. Joe's. Every school had its fervent fans, but theirs were just different. And, over four decades later, I still think they're distinct from everyone else.

My parents remember it a little differently. My mother recalls listening to those early games huddled around our radio. My father remembers watching them in the flickering black and white images of our first television set. But, as I've said, they tend to agree on what's important. St. Joe's was our team, the one the Martellis rooted for.

Whether in person or on radio or TV, I have a lot of memories of Philly sports, pro as well as college. Loyalty dies hard here. I remember going out to the airport to help cheer up the Phillies after they blew the 1964 National League pennant. They were up six and a half games, with only twelve games to play. There was no "wild card." World Series tickets had already been printed. Unfortunately, learning to deal with disappointment also goes into the education of a Philly guy. I was part of a large, supportive crowd. Philly fans don't always boo. They're just more engaged than fans anywhere else. Later I'll recount a story about the 76ers, and a series they actually won. It's been almost a quarter-century since *any* of the major pro teams in Philly won a championship. Some people even say it's because of "Billy Penn's curse," building anything higher than his statue atop City Hall. For decades there had been a "gentleman's agreement" that this would never be done.

But following St. Joe's was still number one. I remember one time they were playing Villanova, an annual confrontation that came to be called the "holy war," only this time it was on a Sunday afternoon. Let's see, wasn't that on January 16, 1966? Whenever I watched or listened to a game that really mattered to me, I used to have this belief that if my team were losing I should turn the game off. Maybe it was all my fault somehow, bad karma.

This time, St. Joe's was being beaten really badly. So I left the house and went over to old Finnegan Playground to shoot hoops by myself, a kind of frigid solace. After a while an older kid I knew came over and said, "Hey, how about St. Joe's?" I was furious. This guy's mocking my team. I had to take him on, big or not. As I charged toward him, he got the picture. "Listen," he said, probably with some expletives added, "St. Joe's won!" Having saved my life, he took off, leaving one fanatical fan to run figure eights all over the court by himself, arms flapping wildly. If I couldn't play, maybe one day I might be their mascot. It turned out that the immortal Steve Donches had sunk a last-second shot to secure the victory, 71 to 69. He wore number 14, like some guy named Jameer about thirty-five years later.

As my father will be happy to tell you, even though I was relatively slow and not the greatest shooter, my teams always seemed to win. That was true on every level I played at, whatever the past history of that particular team or school. I was the starting point guard for our seventh and eighth grade teams, coached by that fine triumvirate of Gallagher, O'Keefe, and Steel. Both years we won our league championship, in seventh grade for the first time in forty-two years.

St. Joseph's Preparatory School is an exceptional institution, with an inspiring history, intertwined with the history of Philadelphia. In my opinion there's no finer high school in the United States. I know a lot about that now. But the reason I wanted to go to the "Prep" for ninth grade was because I believed it might get me into what was then Saint Joseph's College (it didn't become a university until 1978). In fact, originally I was convinced you *had* to graduate from the Prep to be admitted to the college. In a way it's kind of puzzling, since I was beginning to appreciate my limitations as a player, and I surely wanted to play basketball in college. I did know that the Prep was an elite Catholic boy's school, ninth to twelfth grades, located in the heart of the city at 17th and Girard, the academic (and athletic) equivalent of the best independent upper schools in the area for boys.

The fact is, I wasn't entirely wrong. The college and preparatory school were once components of the same institution, founded together by the Jesuits adjacent to old Saint Joseph's Church in the oldest part of Philadelphia. Going from one to the other was still a logical enough progression, but the two had physically and institutionally separated in the nineteenth century—the college relocating in 1927 to a more spacious setting near the suburbs, the Prep staying in the city, adjacent to the impressive Church of the Gesu. It remained a beacon of learning despite the general deterioration of its North Philadelphia neighborhood.

In 1968, finishing eighth grade at St. Philomena, I hadn't even seen the Prep. I didn't need to see it. Mentally I was already there. There was only one problem. It cost more than my parents could afford. But there was also a potential solution. Given my outgoing nature, there can't have been many kids I played with in Lansdowne—or Upper Darby, the adjacent community—who didn't know that Phil Martelli wanted to go to the Prep. As it turned out, a Mr. McKeown, whose son, a Prep student, had died, had established a scholarship to pay the tuition there for worthy applicants. I took the competitive exam for the scholarship and must have done well. I was admitted. Of course, in our household we didn't quite jump for joy, but I'm sure my parents were pleased.

I was on my way, but which way was it? Now I had always walked to school, both in the city and the suburbs. How difficult could it be to find the Prep? All during that summer my father urged me to come ride past the place with him so I could at least see where it was and what it looked like. I didn't care what it looked like. It represented my ticket to the future. I knew there had been a devastating fire at the Prep in 1966, but that the whole place was being rebuilt in the same location.

My mother kept telling me to ask questions, to learn as much as I could about my new school, or even visit it. "Nah," I told both of them, "I'm too busy this summer. Don't worry about it. I'll be all right." After all, I'd grown up in the city. I knew my way around. However much I respected my parents, I saw myself, already a teenager, moving toward independence. And I guess, with the good weather, I wanted to play hoops outdoors every possible day that summer with the friends I'd made. I would've played 365 days a year.

However, by that first exciting morning of my freshman year, I had at least figured out a route to get to the Prep by public transportation. No sweat. Of course, everything went wrong. If you don't know Philadelphia, when you get beyond that ordered core that William Penn laid out so neatly, it's not all that simple, and it's really spread out. It must be fifteen miles or so from Lansdowne to the Girard Avenue location of the school. I took the trolley to 69th Street, then the El (elevated train) to Broad, then the Broad Street Subway all the way to Girard—just about every mode of transportation but a limo. Simple enough, it seemed. Then I actually took my mother's advice. At Broad and Girard, I asked a policeman, the first person I saw, "Can you tell me where St. Joe's Prep is?" He must have thought I was a smartass. Anyway, he told me to go up one light, make a right, and I would walk right into the school. Somehow I missed it, oblivious to where those hundreds of other kids were heading. I wound up at 16th and Montgomery Avenue, only blocks from the school but a world away.

Following the violence and unrest of that summer, September 1968 was a tough time in our country, and especially in North Philadelphia. I was in the wrong place at the wrong moment—a snotty, white prep-school kid in the very heart of the area where serious riots had taken place. But this time I didn't have to ask for directions. An older African-American man sitting on his front steps simply took me by the arm, smiled, and said, "Son, I think you really want to go this way." I guess, as it says in that play, in life we often rely on the kindness of strangers. Sometimes, whatever our age, we should also rely on the foresight of those closest to us, such as our parents. Of course, I was late for my first day of school, and more than a bit disoriented.

Getting home was even more confusing. Growing up in the city, I knew and loved all the complexities of public transportation—subways and buses, all that stuff. But I'd never been east of City Hall, that incredible pile at the very center of everything, Broad and Chestnut Streets. I wound up on an express train, skipping stops, terminating at 8th and Market, nowhere near 69th Street. And I kept making the same mistakes, too flustered to ask for directions. It was like a scene out of *Groundhog Day*. Somehow I eventually found my way back home, hours late. Of course, by then my mother was frightened out of her wits. And so when I was asked, "How did you enjoy your first day at the Prep?" I had to reply, "Fine, I found it." I knew I'd messed up, and should have taken my parents' advice in the first place. Or, as my sister Patti Anne might put it, "You're not in Kansas anymore."

Having recovered my confidence, I somehow convinced Tom Gallagher, my grade-school coach who had become a really close friend, and who actually worked at Broad and Chestnut, to drive me to school every day. Then I managed to get a ride back home to Lansdowne from a fellow student I played basketball with. Yes, some of them had their own cars. They weren't all on scholarship. I may have lost little of my persuasive powers, but the academics at a school like the Prep were really challenging.

Thank heaven for my first coaches—my mother had made me a reader, and my father a hard worker. And, yes, I did play ball, a point guard, of course, and we did achieve success. We'll get into that a bit more. As it turned out, however, in my case the Prep didn't lead directly to Saint Joseph's College. That path would be more circuitous. What the Prep prepared me for was life.

CHAPTER 3

Starting from the Sidelines

PROBABLY THE BEST ADVICE FOR ANYONE UNDERTAKING A NEW venture is from the sage of Stratford-on-Avon in *Hamlet*: "To thine own self be true." Doesn't that just about say it all? If you're true to yourself, how can you be false to others? Of course, Shakespeare also compared the world to a stage on which throughout a lifetime each of us plays many parts. Starting within our own families—our perpetual home team—at times we are leaders, at times learners. The line between the two can be indistinct. I've suggested that each of us is at times a kind of coach, but I don't view my chosen profession as coaching. I'm a teacher.

The court is my classroom. I don't teach plays, I teach people. I learn as much from them as, hopefully, they do from me. If we are effective teachers, we will always learn from those we teach. Growth is possible at any age, and education never ends. In life we do play many parts, and not solely because of how we change with age. Our roles may change more as our experiences and responsibilities broaden our vision.

Which of your teachers, whatever their subject, do you most remember, and why? Some of the specifics of what they imparted may still be retained in the remote recesses of our brains, but isn't it the kind of people they were—or hopefully still are—that really resonates? To be a dedicated teacher is probably the highest calling in life. After all, clergy, too, are teachers. The teachers I remember most vividly, no matter how many years have passed or whether they taught math or man-to-man defense, had qualities we define as character. And so often they were distinctive characters themselves. Maybe that's where I come in.

I met many of these teachers at St. Joseph's Preparatory School. I don't know that I ever fully appreciated what a privilege it was to be there, but I learned to love the Prep—once I figured out how to get there. I had to smile recently when I read a comment purportedly made by their current and very colorful football coach, Gil Brooks. The Prep has long been renowned not only for its academic excellence, but also for its athletic prowess, whether in hoops or crew or football. Even back in the 1920s and '30s they regularly won Catholic League football championships, under another legendary coach named "Ank" Scanlon.

Of the three selective all-boys Catholic high schools in the area, Malvern (which my friend and fellow coach Fran Dunphy attended), La Salle College High School, and St. Joseph's, only the Prep is still based in the heart of Philadelphia. Each tends to do very well in sports. Since it draws students from throughout the region and its perennially powerful football team was once again ranked at the top of the polls in 2006 (until upset by La Salle), the Prep had been accused of unfair advantages in recruiting. "Are you kidding?" Coach Brooks is supposed to have told a reporter, "Of our 900 students, 700 are geeks."

He was probably quoted out of context, as he claimed, but that didn't prevent some newly bespectacled students from showing up at the next game with sweater vests and pocket protectors. Of course, what Brooks was really referring to is how challenging it is, athlete or not, just to get into the Prep. As in my day, you still have to pass a rigorous entrance exam. Moreover, as the school's administrators will attest, the very location of the place can inhibit recruitment. What elite athlete, given the alternative of spacious suburban schools with their state-of-the-art facilities, would chose instead to venture each day into the depths of North Philadelphia, and what parents would choose to expose him to such a supposedly dangerous environment? Even when I attended the Prep decades ago, the surrounding neighborhood was deteriorating. Yet there is something intangible about the place that still makes it so cherished and so popular.

In part, I think it is the very location itself that turns negatives into positives. The character of an institution derives, of course, from the kind of people who make it what it is. After that devastating fire in 1966 had destroyed two-thirds of the Prep's compact campus, the Jesuit fathers, rejecting the preference of many prominent alumni to relocate, decided to rebuild it just where it was. Not only is the Prep's central location still convenient from all directions, it remains a kind of symbol of urban reality to students, many of whom arrive each day from environments of seamless affluence. The Jesuits also serve the surrounding neighborhood, with their Gesu School offering quality education to children, few of whom are Catholic, and many from impoverished homes. The magnificent Church of the Gesu still stands, its edifice reminiscent of Rome, now serving as the Prep's chapel.

I still did well academically at the Prep, although with so much competition I wasn't quite the standout star my parents probably had hoped for. Basketball remained my passion—and yes, the school's varsity team did attain greater success once I took over the point with my methodical game. Playing for a fine coach named Eddie Burke, I like to recall that I was part of a backcourt that averaged thirty points a game. I don't always add that Mo Howard scored twenty-eight of them.

My parents continued to come to every game. It meant a lot to me, largely unspoken but understood. I still think about it today when I see my father up there at the top of the stands, not only at every game but also at every practice. You can't put a price on that. The Prep's basketball tradition continues today under the skilled leadership of yet another authentically legendary character, William "Speedy" Morris, formerly the head coach of both the men's and women's teams at La Salle University. He has been known to do standup comedy.

Although I attended high school miles away from home, I never completely lost contact with the kids in my suburban neighborhood. I even began my coaching career with young parish teams, trying to give back to those who had nurtured my own love for the game and repay those older kids who had included me wherever they went. As I never get tired of saying, there's a kind of unique equity about basketball, a game that transcends every barrier—economic, neighborhood, racial, and religious.

It's funny what you remember. I must have been about twelve when Tom Gallagher took me to my first professional game at the old Convention Hall in West Philadelphia. It's no longer there, and in fact, even expanded and modernized, it wasn't really an ideal venue for viewing sports or much of anything else. Yet so many memorable events took place there. In 1948, its smoke-filled arena was the setting for three presidential nominations, the only time in history that three major political conventions were held in the same place during the same summer.

Well, that night, the Philadelphia 76ers, led by the great (no, I won't say "legendary" again) Wilt Chamberlain faced the San Francisco Warriors (formerly of Philadelphia), led by sharpshooting Rick Barry, in the pivotal fifth game of the final series for the NBA championship. Despite the fact that the game had long since been sold out, Tom said not to worry. He "knew a guy" (shades of Grandfather Martelli). We did meet someone outside, I'm not sure by prearrangement. I now know that he was a scalper, but he wasn't so much selling tickets as selling access. He didn't look all that mysterious, just a regular guy, although he kept glancing rather nervously around. Tom asked him how much. "Five bucks," the guy replied. "And how much for the kid?" No reduced rates—it was five bucks for me as well. So Tom gave him ten dollars. Then we followed him down an alley, where he popped open a manhole cover. We went down into the bowels underneath the Convention Center, and somehow emerged inside the building. (Imagine doing that today in the airtight environs of the Wachovia Center or the Spectrum.) I've heard of knothole gangs at old ballparks, but never getting into a basketball game by going underground.

I told that story at Tom's memorial service—and, yes, people laughed as they tend to do for those they knew and loved who die too soon. Probably more than a few of the mourners may have believed I made it up. Of course, it's true, and not all that different from other events I got to, one way or another, because of the generous people I met through sports. Unfortunately, Tom and I didn't have seats, and the place was predictably packed. After we emerged from the underworld, we just walked around the corridors and watched the game. Ten bucks for standing room, in 1960s currency, but it was worth it, even though the Sixers lost that night. They went on to win the series, but this was not a frequent-enough phenomenon in Philly, then or now.

Despite the fact that I'd played well at the Prep, there was certainly nothing flashy about my game. I was a distributor, happy to bring the ball down-court, still neither fast afoot nor much of a shooter. "A coach on the court," at least in my own mind, and hopefully my coach's. I was not heavily recruited by colleges. I knew I hadn't the credentials to play competitive Division I college ball, certainly not on the level of Saint Joseph's. But, after all, as I'd announced to Stevie Stefano back in eighth grade, my ultimate goal was less to play up on Hawk Hill than to coach there. Still, I definitely wanted to play somewhere, and the best opportunity seemed to be in Division III.

One small Catholic college in Ohio had expressed interest in me. Somehow my father found the time to drive me all the way out there to see them. I tell people today that I can make the time to do whatever I feel is important, no matter how busy my schedule happens to be. Some of that must come from my father, to whom hard work was a constant. The love of reading came from my mother, but we must have been a bit light in the geography department. Dad and I had gone some three hundred miles on the Pennsylvania Turnpike, and yet we were still in the Keystone State. Just how far could the Ohio border be? My heart sank at the prospect of attending college so far from home. My father recalls sensing that sentiment with every passing mile.

When we finally got to the campus, outside of Columbus, I was almost relieved to find that the situation just didn't seem right to me. The people there couldn't have been nicer, but, as I saw it, their coach was limited by an approach that was so realistic that it was almost negative. I think we'll win our share of games, he said, even if not a championship. I wondered, why rule it out at the start? I'd been surrounded by optimistic people in my playing career thus far. I may not have been a prime recruit, but I already had the conviction that to be good at anything, you had to strive to be great. My teams on every level had overachieved, had gone beyond prudent projections, and I wanted to play for a college that also reached for the top.

I found the right setting, as luck would have it, only a few miles from home, in Chester, Pennsylvania, at what was then called Widener College. A remarkable man, the late F. Eugene Dixon, Jr., whom everyone knew as "Fitz," had guided its transformation from a small school, the major component of which had been the Pennsylvania Military College, to what eventually became, as the brochures say, "a flourishing, four-campus multidisciplinary metropolitan university."

Heir to the immense Widener fortune, Dixon invested his millions and his time in an astonishing variety of organizations and charities, from hospitals to schools. Something of a character himself, he may have been a Philadelphia equivalent of "the happiest millionaire." His special interests were education and sports. He taught and coached for years at Episcopal Academy, which he had attended prior to going to Harvard, and he must have been on the boards of a dozen other academic institutions. At one time, Dixon owned all or part of Philadelphia's professional basketball, ice hockey, and indoor lacrosse teams, and he raised horses. I suppose his interest and influence in Widener may have stemmed from the desire to have an enduring monument to the prominent family whose heritage was now his to represent. Heads of two prior generations of Wideners had perished together on the *Titanic*. It's quite a story. Dixon's father had married into the family, and Fitz became the caretaker of its resources.

I'm not quite sure how I was first steered to Widener, but it was probably through one of those young coaches who had befriended me. I do know that my father and I both met Fitz Dixon. He didn't simply head their board and pump in money, but was very much a hands-on presence during that time at Widener. He loved being around the campus and meeting its students personally. As always, my father recalls it a bit differently than I do. In his version, somehow we actually had lunch with Dixon in the Widener cafeteria, and after he discovered both my love of basketball and our inability to pay the school's tuition, Fitz told us the equivalent of "don't worry about anything." That would have been great had it happened, but it never did. After all, I wasn't exactly a Billy "White Shoes" Johnson, who played football for Widener and went on to a spectacular career in the NFL. I was just plain young Phil Martelli, a kid hooked on hoops who hopefully had some potential to play the point for their Division III basketball team.

I think I first met Dixon at a Widener football game, where you could hear his voice exhorting their players from just about any part of the stands. What I am certain of is that I did receive some financial assistance to attend the school, whoever initiated and put it together. The package included outright aid, student loans, and work-study—but many students had something similar to this. I'm sure my parents sacrificed a good deal to make up the difference and see me through college. As usual, there was not a word about it from them. When, twenty-eight years after I graduated, I received an honorary degree from Widener and addressed the graduates of 2004 from the same stands, and I talked about fulfilling their own dreams and the nature of leadership, my parents were never far from my mind.

The coaches at Widener validated my conviction that it's OK to pursue championships. Under head coach Alan Rowe, that was always our aim. Many college programs are preoccupied with wins, sometimes even modest wins, as a measure of success. At Widener, whether in football or basketball, they always talked about achieving championships. Coach Rowe was also fanatical about preparation. Being fully prepared is half the battle. Years later, when I met John Wooden, I was reminded of how calmly he had coached, rolled-up program in hand. The really

Little Angel. My First Communion. *Courtesy of the Martelli family*

Little Devil. "Meet me at the Dairy Queen." *Courtesy of the Martelli family*

Still my coaches: Philip Edgar and Mary Jane Martelli. *Courtesy of the Martelli family*

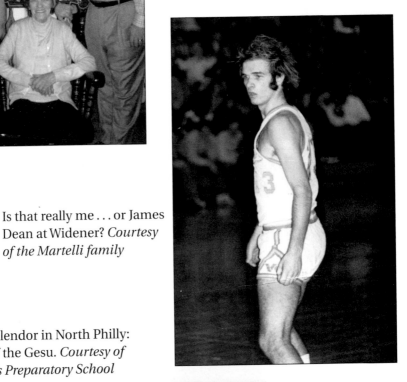

Is that really me . . . or James Dean at Widener? *Courtesy of the Martelli family*

Roman splendor in North Philly: Church of the Gesu. *Courtesy of St. Joseph's Preparatory School*

What it's all about: Dwayne Lee, Dave Mallon, and Chet Stachitas at Commencement, 2006. *Courtesy of Saint Joseph's University.*

Wedding bells: Judy and our three children. *Courtesy of the Martelli family*

Clare Ariano between John Griffin and his successor. *Courtesy of Sideline Photos/ Saint Joseph's University*

Height of Hawk Hill: Barbelin Hall. *Courtesy of Saint Joseph's University*

Timothy R. Lannon, S.J., President of Saint Joseph's University. *Courtesy of Saint Joseph's University*

"Bo": Jim Boyle willing a win. *Courtesy of Saint Joseph's University*

"Oh When the Hawks Go Flying In!" *Courtesy of Sideline Photos/Saint Joseph's University*

Our second home: Palestra pandemonium! *Courtesy of Sideline Photos/Saint Joseph's University*

There is a serious side to what I do . . . *Courtesy of Sideline Photos/ Saint Joseph's University*

. . . but it can be so satisfying. *Courtesy of Sideline Photos/ Saint Joseph's University*

Rashid Bey. *Courtesy of Saint Joseph's University*

Dmitri Domani. *Courtesy of Saint Joseph's University*

Terrell Myers. *Courtesy of Saint Joseph's University*

Marvin O'Connor. *Courtesy of Saint Joseph's University*

Bill Phillips. *Courtesy of Saint Joseph's University*

Tyrone Barley. *Courtesy of Saint Joseph's University*

hard work of preparation had been completed before his teams took the floor. It isn't all that different in any walk of life. I remember reading that Alfred Hitchcock viewed the actual filming of his memorable movies as the easiest part of the process. The real work was done earlier, carefully plotting every detail of every scene before the cameras ever rolled. But he viewed actors as essentially props, a view I've never held of my players.

I also learned a lot from my teammates, some of whom became very close friends and have influenced what I've done and how I've done it, on and off the court. Two who stand out are Jim Hargadon, now chief financial officer for Okidata, and Pat Knapp, currently the women's basketball coach for the University of Pennsylvania. Because of the attitude of our coaches and the commitment of our players, we *did* play for championships. We vied for the championship of our league in my very first season and won it in both my junior and senior years. Being in Division III (where they actually have football playoffs, as well) doesn't make the competition any less heated. Far from it—look at the few Division III games you can see on television.

In my senior year we were highly ranked nationally, and our record justified it. We played in the East Regional against the University of Scranton in their arena, to go to the Final Four. It turned out to be my last college game. Alan Rowe was a fierce competitor, but always under control. As I'll note later, he taught me a valuable lesson about temperament. In the four years I played for him, he was never nailed with a technical foul. Yet he received one in this game for some mysterious infraction. He hadn't said or done anything to merit it, so far as I or any of the other Widener players or partisans in attendance could see.

Unfortunately, there were very few of them in the house. My college years coincided with the severe gas shortage brought about by some newly powerful organization called OPEC. It probably came as a mixed blessing to my siblings, limiting the away games that our parents could drag them to. Sometimes you could only get gas for your car every other day, and in modest quantities. Of course, my father found a solution. On those days when he couldn't get any gas and we were going upstate, he would simply ride with us on the team bus. The coaches didn't mind having him along. Although very genial, he didn't bombard them with advice, any more than he does to me today, but he was an unconditional supporter of our team, and vocally brutal to referees. Never more so than when they made that call so blatantly unfair in his opinion that it all but labeled them "homers." Who was paying them off?

Maybe a second or so after Coach Rowe got his "T," my dad launched himself out of the stands, went directly to the scorer's table, and started loudly berating the refs. They hardly knew what to do about it. Just who was this guy? So they did what came naturally. They blew their whistles and dramatically announced that the game would not continue until this lunatic was put out of the gym. There must have been about 6,000 Scranton fans there, and not many more on our side than the twelve of us on the team. Two security guards who couldn't have been much older than eighteen put their hands on my father and started steering him behind the bench to escort him out. Now, my teammate and roommate was a tough Vietnam veteran in his twenties named Tommy Mann. He turned to the two young guys and said in an even voice, "You better get your hands off of him." They mouthed off in reply, and suddenly there was a skirmish that threatened to escalate into a riot. A few of us kept our heads and stopped it.

At odds of 6,000 to little more than twelve, we weren't going to win any battles, nor did we win that game. My father went out the door on his own, simply walked through the lobby, came back in through the other door, and quietly watched the rest of the contest. Yes, he managed to get to every game, from my seventh-grade team on, but he never ceased yelling at referees until in my first year of coaching high-school ball, when I finally had to ask him to please stop. His support is no less inhibited today and no less appreciated—just quieter.

I loved Widener, just as I'd loved the Prep. Maybe I'm one of those peculiar people who simply like the structure of school. I also had the advantage in college of not being a commuter. I lived in a fraternity house with about twenty other guys, and really enjoyed campus life. Of course, Widener was much smaller in the transitional 1970s than it is today. It became a university shortly after I graduated.

The school had some unusual features. The whole place would simply shut down for the entire month of January. I'm not sure precisely why. And twice during our four years we had to participate in a sort of mini-session involving intensive study of a practical subject far removed from our major. Mine was political science, and I thought for a time about going on to study law. However, my goal of coaching basketball prevailed. You can't major in that, at least not at legitimate universities like Widener. In fact, by now my ambition had progressed to a specific time frame. The path would start by coaching in high school and becoming a head coach by the age of twenty-five. I wanted to be a college assistant by the time I was thirty, and a head coach on that level by the age of thirty-five. So, as it turned out, I missed some marks.

The two mini-session courses I selected would be of considerable benefit to me later on. The first was learning how to prepare a federal income-tax form. As a result, until I could afford professional assistance, I did my own taxes. Somehow I never got audited. The second session proved even more relevant—learning all about athletic training. One semester, I suppose because I'd taken on extra work earlier, I had no classes at all. I recall that during that January, when the campus was dormant with just about everyone gone except for the basketball players, I checked out every book in the college library that had anything to do with coaching. I accumulated a stack of books next to my bed and read them every night—the Abe Lincoln of Widener, only with the blessings of electricity. Fortunately, what I didn't have in my room were the diversions of a television set or stereo. Some of what I read went back to the very beginnings of basketball.

You may be aware that unlike baseball, our "national pastime," and football, our "national passion," we know how, when, and where the sport of basketball began, and the man who originated it—James Naismith, in 1891. It's fascinating how it developed, and how universally popular it has become. I kept a notebook about what I'd read, things that made sense to me, and things that didn't. I was hardly a bookworm in college, but I was trying to gather all the specific knowledge I could for the profession I intended to pursue.

There were, however, more immediate pursuits. Between my junior and senior years, I was enthralled by the exploits of a local basketball team from a college much smaller than Widener that was actually winning national championships. It was in something called the AIAW, not yet the NCAA, but that didn't make any difference. They weren't young men; they were the remarkable young women of Immaculata College. Long before women's basketball achieved anything remotely approaching the visibility it enjoys today, they were a Philly phenomenon. Immaculata didn't have its own arena, but they would sell out local high-school and college gyms as large as Villanova's fieldhouse. They drew a full house just about everywhere they played. We used to listen to their games on the radio, all of us gathered around a set at the fraternity house, avidly following "girls'" basketball. Imagine, a national power in our back yard.

Even while playing at Widener, I continued to coach youth basketball. I also went out of my way to get to know everyone I could who was involved in the game. Although we didn't call it that at the time, I was really networking. One significant acquaintance I made was an already very highly regarded local sportswriter named Dick Weiss. He now writes out of New York, his middle name universally acknowledged as "Hoops." He was then following the Immaculata team, the most appealing sports story in town. I knew they had a summer camp teaching basketball to girls up in the Poconos, and Weiss arranged for me to get an interview to work there as a counselor. That it was an all-female camp didn't exactly diminish its appeal. As it turned out, I met there the two women who would change my life. It may be more accurate to say that they made it possible.

I think that Cathy Rush, the head coach at Immaculata and director of the camp, all but founded women's basketball as we think of it today. I hope that by the time this book is published, she will finally have been nominated for her rightful place in the Naismith Memorial Basketball Hall of Fame in Springfield, Massachusetts. It's great that a film is being made about her exploits. She had a tremendous influence on me, really getting me zeroed in on organization. Until I met Cathy, my knowledge was largely theoretical. I'm proud of the way I organize today, but it was Cathy who explained to me the concept of turning practice into an ongoing program and not merely a team. More than generous with her time, she was also thoughtful and considerate. So was Hoops Weiss, who'd asked another counselor to keep an eye out for me, since I probably wouldn't know anyone up there.

Despite my difficulty with directions, however, I actually found the Poconos and the camp. As I drove into the grounds and got out of my car, the first person I saw was this blonde vision, sitting all by herself on the porch of the main building. Her name, I soon discovered, was Judy Marra. She was a student at Immaculata, a member of Cathy's team, and the one Hoops soon introduced me to. Good choice. Judy wasn't quite one of Immaculata's stars, but

I soon discovered she could shoot a basketball a lot more accurately than I could. I should write a line here about shooting arrows instead. On my part it was love at first sight. By the end of camp, in August, I like to think it was reciprocal.

With my memory, it's fortunate that the most important occasions in my life have coincided with sporting events. Our first official date was on Labor Day weekend, when I recall we attended the Penn State-Temple football game at Franklin Field. Two months later, in November 1975, I asked Judy to marry me. Officially, I asked her father for her hand on the day in January 1976 when the Flyers beat that powerful touring Russian team. To get his undivided attention, I made my request between the first and second periods. I graduated from Widener in May 1976, and Judy and I were married that November. That we've lived happily ever after is due to many factors, in large part her patience, forbearance, and good sense. But it doesn't hurt that she really understands what I do for a living, why I do it, and what its demands mean for a family.

CHAPTER 4

Heading Up to Hawk Hill

YES, I'M FORTUNATE TO BE MARRIED TO JUDY, AS THE PROFES-sors say, on many levels. You can't make it in any profession without a supportive family. That is nowhere more true than in coaching or teaching. In those early years of our marriage, Judy was more than supportive. She understood as only a colleague could. Although she worked full-time for a bank in Center City Philadelphia, she also served as assistant coach for the women's basketball team at Villanova. Since they practiced at night, I would often be coming home just as she would be leaving. You might say that sometimes we weren't really sure if either of us was coming or going.

No matter how deeply devoted to each other, all newlyweds have struggles—trying to make ends meet, learning to compromise, deciding when to start a family. Getting married itself is a challenge, beyond which everyone is tested, whatever the circumstances. Many times I thought about the road not taken.

Perhaps I should have followed the only other career path I'd seriously considered—building on my Widener political science degree to go to law school, and after a hopefully productive practice, maybe going into politics myself. I might have wound up writing the foreword to a book by Ed Rendell instead of the other way around. It would take a good many more years than I'd projected to justify that original career choice I'd vowed to pursue all the way back in the eighth grade.

So far as I know, no one actually majors in coaching (although I've seen some pretty peculiar majors listed while watching college sports on television). It's a track you set for yourself. I think I already understood in college that most of all coaching is teaching. It may be that I also wanted the security of something else to fall back on, just in case, but my parallel major of secondary education led to the certification that would prove awfully helpful later on. Learning as much as I could from what I saw, what I'd experienced, and what I'd read all those nights in my room filled in my own course of study as a future coach. When the opportunity came, I had to be prepared. I was pretty certain the paths I'd taken would lead to that opportunity, but it would be up to me to take advantage of it.

Of course, I still had a lot to learn, which you can only do on the job, but it seemed clear that in coaching at any level temperament is more important than technique. Whether coaching those grade-school teams when I was back at the Prep or kids my own age in independent summer leagues when I was at Widener, one motivation was to give back to all the people who had given so generously to me. But I also wanted to see what worked and what didn't—not just the plays and patterns, but *how* to motivate. If you don't know how to do that, you can't accomplish very much, no matter how much knowledge you have.

I'd learned particularly at Widener how important it was for both players and coaches to handle themselves in any situation.

What we did, and how we conducted our business around the campus, was reflected in how we acted on the floor. I think there was a moment when I moved mentally from player to coach, a painful experience at the time that later proved invaluable. Although I'd hardly been a standout star heavily recruited to play college ball, I still had something in me of that brash kid who had once been dumped into a trash can. I was still a bit cocky and outspoken at Widener, on and off the court.

Despite my high regard for our head coach, during my senior year I mouthed off after a particularly galling loss, blaming him in front of my teammates for too much substituting. As the season progressed, not surprisingly, I didn't play as much as I had earlier in my college career. Yet, miraculously, the team did very well, and even with fewer minutes I think I contributed at least as much to our success as I had previously. After so blatantly overstepping my bounds as a player, the coach had more than good reason to throw me off the team, but he didn't. We settled it privately, I never popped off again, and neither his stature nor our relationship was severed.

Ironically, that mistake I'd made in college came back the other way around during my first year as the head coach of Saint Joseph's. A player challenged my strategy after an early-season loss—in our locker room, in front of everyone. My first reaction was to throw *him* off the team, but then I thought back to my own experience as a college senior. Instead, we talked it out man-to-man. There are times when we all think we know too much. I told him I valued his advice, but that wasn't the time or place to voice it. Our goals were the same, to succeed. There was no recurrence of that outburst, and he helped us to a winning season. Sometimes we all have to take a step back, even the person in charge.

The foundation of everything I've learned about coaching, although incubated when I myself was still a student, comes from being a high-school coach. When I became engaged as a senior in college, after giving Judy her ring, all I lacked was a job. She knew I wanted to coach, and hoped also to teach. It was all that networking that got me started, along with a little necessary initiative.

I had met Bud Gardler at a camp after my freshman year in college, and knew he had been a successful high-school coach. The world of basketball may lack the stability of, say, the world of accounting, but once you gain entry, you keep running into a lot of the same people. What changes is what they're doing and where they happen to be doing it. Bud had gone to Washington to coach at American University, but was back in the Philly area to take over the program at Cardinal O'Hara High School. Since we'd already worked together, I didn't feel awkward sending him a letter, and he agreed to let me be the JV coach there. My ultimate destination might be distant, but at least now I was headed in the right direction.

I also got a teaching job, at an elementary school called St. Martin of Tours. Fortunately, the Catholic Church has so many saints that it will never run out of names for its schools. Now, you have to know Greater Philadelphia to appreciate the logistical challenges involved. Judy and I lived in an apartment in suburban Clifton Heights in a building owned by her father. He was good enough to take the rent money we paid and put it in escrow for our first house. We really learned how to budget, not that there was very much to budget with. We also learned how to allocate that other important commodity, our time.

St. Martin of Tours, on Roosevelt Boulevard in the appropriately named Far Northeast of Philadelphia, was some thirty miles from our apartment, about forty-five minutes by car. O'Hara is down near Springfield, in suburban Delaware County. So I'd leave Clifton Heights around dawn, go to where I taught, then another forty-five minutes to where I coached, and then, thankfully, only about fifteen minutes to get home just in time to see my wife take off for Villanova. It must have been at least a hundred miles every day. I didn't know if she could cook until we'd been married for a few years.

I had no retrospective complaints. You have to pay your dues pursuing any profession you believe in enough to hang with it. And it helps to take the long view, sometimes even the long drive. But when I hear today how overpaid we high-profile head coaches are in Division I basketball, I can only smile. I made the odd total of $4,999 for these two jobs I held initially. I drove a green Vega that seemed to consume more oil than gas. I don't recall running out in the middle of a busy intersection, as I had with my first car, but sometimes I wondered if, all things considered, I wound up with any net profit at all. I did this for two years. Eventually I got smart and instead of going back to coach at O'Hara, I managed to get a job as an assistant coach back at Widener. Of course, I knew I'd be less geographically challenged if I could do all my work at one location. However, I'd learned a lot at O'Hara, a good program on the high-school level. There isn't a job you undertake that you won't learn from.

Step two of that four-step Martelli master plan was to be a head coach in the highly competitive Philadelphia Catholic League by the time I was twenty-five. I had no prejudice against other school systems. This was simply the environment I'd been raised in, and knew best. How many accounts of people's lives begin with, "As it turned out . . ."? The timing of opportunities may be a accidental, but, again, we have to be positioned to take advantage of them.

Well, as it turned out, the head coaching position at Bishop Kenrick High School's basketball program did come open. Bud Gardler, who had given me my first job, had been Kenrick's very successful head coach. The school's principal, formerly its basketball moderator and chaplain, held a high opinion of Gardler. So I'd another incentive to apply for the job. I was all of twenty-three, but I knew enough to thoroughly prepare for my interview. I had to allay their fears of hiring someone so young. I must have done a good job of presenting myself because I got the job. Unfortunately, the interview itself was my most successful example of preparation that year. Talking a good game won't win it.

The fact is, I probably *was* too young. Looking back, I think I made the mistake of being too caught up in what I viewed as the prestige of the position. That is why to this day I want to be recognized more for the job that I do than the title I have. I was a really bad coach. I didn't organize my team practice by practice. I didn't organize each practice minute by minute, as I do today. As I said at the outset of this book, you have to be egotistical to be an effective coach. You have to believe in what you're telling people to do. But that confidence has to be based on substance, and substance is based on experience. Overconfidence masking insecurity will lead to disaster.

If possible, I may have tried too hard in that first year at Kenrick. I did listen to a lot of people. I wasn't yet really comfortable with my own opinions, or my ability to express them, whether in dealing with players or designing plays. I was guilty of just about everything a coach, or teacher, can do wrong—not communicating clearly, not being fully prepared, not being organized, with very little clarity and nothing you could call a vision of where we wanted to go as a team. The result was a wall of uncertainty separating me from the kids I'd been hired to coach. Sometimes the pressures made me almost irrational and overly demonstrative, especially during games. I must have had seven technicals that season.

But through it all, I kept learning. It just didn't pay off until later. There are times to this day when I see in my mind some of the guys I coached that year. I wasn't much older than they were. They're probably now in their mid-forties. I still feel bad about letting them down. They were talented enough to win more. Kenrick meant as much to them as the Prep meant to me. But I wasn't a good enough coach at the time—too volatile, too irrational, too unpredictable. I learned at their expense. My mistake at the start may have been to seek too much advice, resulting in too many differing opinions. I knew I needed help from someone who could put it all together.

"How did your first season go?" Cathy Rush asked me that summer. "Not very well," I was honest enough to reply. She asked to see my game plans. I hadn't any to show her. That would be the last time I didn't have any plans for my teams. She might have said, "Have you forgotten so soon everything I taught you?" Instead, she meticulously laid it all out for me again—but with this year of head-coaching experience, however disjointed, behind me, I was able to see it all so much more clearly. If I pride myself on anything today, it is how thoroughly I plan every minute of every practice, almost every minute of every day, so that I'll never be unprepared again. As John Wooden put it, "Failing to prepare is preparing to fail." Were I given to putting things this way, I might say that the three most important "P's" in doing any job well are *preparation*, not losing your *perspective*, and not *prejudging* others.

I learned a great lesson that first year at Kenrick about prejudging other people. It also says a lot about perseverance, a fourth "P." I cut a kid named Johnny Custer, a sophomore. He was only five-foot-four, and just didn't seem big enough to make much of a contribution to our team. The next day he came back to practice and asked if he could be a team manager for the year. He just wanted to be around the program. Johnny was a very thorough person, and he did a fine job. The following year he came back and made the junior varsity. Then he came back as a senior, finally made the varsity, was elected team captain, was named all-league, went on to play college ball, and moved on to a productive career.

I've always told the story of Johnny Custer's perseverance whenever I make public appearances. In my first season as head coach on Hawk Hill, he called me on the phone to thank me for remembering him. One of his friends had heard one of my talks. I asked him why, as a kid of fifteen, he had come back at Kenrick just to be a team manager. He replied, "It was always my goal to play for my high-school team. More important, I thought that the guys you kept must have something that I didn't have, and I had to be there every day to study it."

At Saint Joseph's we always have open practices. During that dream season, 2003–04, you can imagine what they were like. We try to be accommodating to everybody, but at the end of practices that season, coaches and players alike would go more quickly than usual to the locker room so that we all wouldn't be bombarded for yet one more interview, or a dozen more autographs, and the like. That particular day, nearly a decade after his memorable call to me, I glimpsed Johnny at practice out of the corner of my eye. He'd brought his son, his nephew, and his brother to watch it with him. Afterwards, I heard a knock on my office door. It was Johnny. We made amiable small talk, and as he left, he turned around. Anticipating his question, I said, "The answer's 'yes.'" I still tell his story everywhere I go, but now it's more powerful than ever.

The longer I stayed at Kenrick, the more I learned. Any team is formed by many separate parts, not simply the person who guides it. For a young kid to have the perseverance to believe in himself, to maintain and achieve his goals, can't fail but make an impact on his coach. If a team is made up of many parts, so too is a person. Whatever I've become today is a composite of all the players I've learned from.

Talk about not prejudging—later at Kenrick, I yelled at a player named Mark Bernsteil and yanked him out of a game because he just wasn't responding to my directions on the court.

Later his mother explained to me that he couldn't hear out of one ear. It may be he hadn't told me because of peer pressure. Kids challenge each other constantly, and a coach has to be sensitive enough to be aware of it. Hopefully, you'll ultimately achieve a harmony out of that thing we call team chemistry. This is probably even more vital in high school than in college, and more important in college than in the pros.

I think it takes more skill to coach young kids, with not yet fully formed personalities, than to deal with the mega-millionaires who populate professional basketball, but there are more similarities than differences. Brilliant high-school coaches like Bob Hurley or Morgan Wooten would, I'm convinced, be just as successful on the college level. Brilliant coaches of women's college teams like Pat Summitt or Geno Auriemma would be just as successful coaching men. Of course, many college coaches have had success in the NBA, although circumstances can be as important as skill. There may be giant egos to contend with, often including the ownership, but at least you don't have to recruit every year. And, given a good interpreter, I believe the right kind of coach could be successful almost anywhere in the world, now that basketball vies with soccer as the most international of sports. Consider how many foreign players have been successful on both the college and professional levels in the United States, their numbers increasing every year—and how many young Americans are playing on teams throughout the world, often learning the language as they go along.

During my high-school coaching experience, I not only learned most of what I know, I believe I got better at my craft. Success is measured by more than wins alone, but by my second year at Kenrick, we played for the Catholic League championship. Although losing to a Roman Catholic High School powerhouse coached by Speedy Morris, we went on to make the playoffs six times in a row—a school record. We were becoming something of a powerhouse ourselves.

Of course, the Martelli master plan was to become a college assistant coach by the age of thirty. Early in this account I noted that I don't really have a lot of firm friends of such long duration as my parents do, and suggested that my pursuit of basketball may have something to do with this. What I had most in common with many of my friends from high school and college was that we played on the same teams. I had great times with my fraternity brothers in college, but it was largely a social thing. I'd be happy to see a lot of these guys again, but if you asked me if I have lifelong friends from college, it would be stretching it to name even two.

On the other hand, some of my closest friends today are also clustered around basketball, and our mutual interests go far beyond that. I first met Geno Auriemma at Cathy Rush's camp. I believe that over the years at least a hundred of the people who served on her staff, both women and men, have gone on to coach the women's game in college. I was a bit unusual in that I came to be a counselor, and eventually the camp director, while I was coaching boys in high school. Geno had the same sort of career path in mind. He wanted to start out as a high-school teacher and coach, preferably in the Catholic League, where he too had grown up. At the time, he was still a student at West Chester, pursuing his degree and stocking shelves at a grocery store after school.

One summer night, after our camp chores were done, I said, "Why don't you help me at Kenrick? I could use an assistant." There wasn't much money in it, but it certainly served his own career objectives, and Kenrick was his alma mater. For the next two years we were inseparable, exchanging ideas, going to Phillies games, or just hanging out—two kindred spirits, although very different personalities, with the same objectives in

CHAPTER 5

Coaching Is Primarily about Character

T HIS IS NOT ONLY WHAT I BELIEVE, IT'S THE HEADLINE OF AN article I wrote for the *Philadelphia Inquirer* in November 2003. After there had been a series of unfortunate incidents involving the men's basketball programs at several major universities, the National Association of Basketball Coaches took the unprecedented step of calling together all the Division I coaches for a meeting in suburban Chicago to address issues of ethics and professionalism. It wasn't sufficient to point out how few schools had been involved in such incidents, or how many more pervasive examples of corruption and exploitation there probably are in other areas of American life. Each of us came out of that meeting committed to doing a better job as coaches, as teachers, and hopefully as role models.

As I wrote at the time, "How powerful it is for young people to have a voice in their mind and heart that says, 'I want to be like my coach.' Bottom line: Coaching is about our character and the character we can develop in those we teach." I may not always have lived up to such lofty sentiments, but I surely had role models of my own to emulate—from my school and college coaches to Cathy Rush to the remarkable series of men who preceded me at St. Joe's. What they all had in common was character.

The basketball program at what is now Saint Joseph's University will soon celebrate its centennial. The first men's team to take the floor in our name was in 1909, only eighteen years after the founding of the sport itself. By the way, their record was 10 and 6. The longest tenure of any of our coaches, a full quarter of that century, has been that of Bill Ferguson. He was so successful, especially with his celebrated "Mighty Mites" team of the 1930s (averaging only five-foot-ten in height) that the college yearbook proclaimed, "Notre Dame had its Rockne, Saint Joseph's has its Bill Ferguson." With his "home" court over at St. Joseph's Prep, Ferguson's teams accumulated an overall record of just under .600.

Unfortunately, I never got to meet Bill, but he and I do have something in common. Ferguson was a 1920 graduate of the University of Pennsylvania. Of the coaches who succeeded him, all were Saint Joseph's graduates until the incumbent. Consider their names, and their legacy. What a group of distinctive personalities. They include the cerebral Dr. Jack Ramsay with his unmatched winning percentage of .765, the ebullient Jack McKinney (who coached all-Americans Cliff Anderson and Mike Bantom), Harry Booth, and Jim Lynam. Imagine, I now worked the same sidelines.

Naturally enough, I think most of all about my two immediate predecessors, who but for their shared integrity could hardly have been more different: Jim Boyle, the "Bo" who embraced life, and John Griffin, the intense competitor who personified loyalty. It was Boyle who brought me up to Hawk Hill, the ultimate destination I'd envisioned since childhood, during that wonderful season of 1985–86, his fifth at the helm. What a year it was. Only one prior team had won twenty-six games—a team coached by "Dr. Jack," of course, over twenty years before. It looked like we had a dynasty going, and I would be part of it.

Jim Boyle, who passed away at the end of 2005 after a battle with lung cancer, is a hard person to recapture with words. He taught me what it meant to be a Hawk, in every aspect of life, with basketball being only the point of departure. He had the unique ability to make you think and question, just as he did virtually every day of his sixty-three years. He turned what too often could be a "me" profession into a "we" profession of sharing—with everyone who worked with him, perhaps most of all his family. He was the ultimate family man. His wife, Tess, was really involved in the program. His children, one of whom went to Harvard and the other three to Saint Joseph's, were very involved as well, beyond simply being proud of their father. It was a daily lesson to me, then with young children of my own, that you can be consumed with your job without sacrificing or separating yourself from those you love. It's not easy to include your family in everything you do. Bo would constantly ask them, and us, our impressions of a situation or a player. It was no act. He was genuinely interested in what we had to say. In a selfish world, he was truly selfless.

And what an innovative, inquisitive mind. Bo was the first person I knew who was really into videotape. He studied our opponents ceaselessly, and if there was one area in which he was really demanding of us assistant coaches, it was that we promptly provided him with all the videotape we could possibly obtain. In addition, he watched every game he could on television. To this day, I can't get enough information about our opponents, anything that might give us an edge.

Yet Jim Boyle had unique, almost instinctive views on recruiting that sometimes made him seem more like a guru. He would look at body types and tell you whether he thought that the kid was going to be a good player, without actually seeing him play. It wasn't based on anything as obvious as height or weight. Bo might look at a kid's ears, or consider just the way he walked, even something like an excess of body hair. I mean, we weren't exactly picking America's top model. Yet for whatever reasons, his instincts frequently proved out on the court.

Bo's first love was his family, then his school, but he was interested in just about everything. "Eclectic" hardly describes it. He always wanted to learn more, whether it was chess or the nature of the Chinese language. He *had* to know everything about it, once a certain subject caught his fancy. And he'd talk about it in a way that was fascinating, whether you shared his new passion or not. It seemed obsessive, but retrospectively I think he was trying to deflect the pressures that come with this job by losing himself in something entirely different for a time, a sort of daily vacation of the mind.

Our dynasty didn't last long. We started to lose the very next season, despite all his preparation, all the tapes, all the motivation. Things bottomed out in the 1989–90 season when Bo's team won only seven games and lost twenty-one. Overall, his nine years had been more than successful, but after that season he resigned. Losing was hard enough, but it was more than problems on the court. A kind of separation at Saint Joseph's had developed that is hard to imagine today, between its academic and athletic constituencies. Bo, whose interests encompassed both realms, was caught in the middle of it.

Hard as it was to go through all this at his side, I learned from Bo even during that agonizing season. His successful teams had not developed, for whatever reasons, into a consistently successful program, positioned for future success. I vowed that were I ever in his position, I would choose more carefully what battles to fight, confining such contests to what most directly affected my teams, not undertaking more than I could manage. Even then, Bo helped prepare me for my own ultimate opportunity.

Yes, we head coaches may seem overcompensated at times, but this is a trying and demanding business. I think in the end that Bo, who so loved everything Saint Joseph's represented, left most of all because of his family. It's ironic; in effect, his great strength did him in. No coach had involved his family more in the pursuit of his profession, so it hurt even more when his wife and kids had also to endure the snide remarks and outright hostility of the fans in the stands, once things went bad. Being so intimately involved, Tess and the children weren't about to stay home. Bo could take it, but why should they have to?

Certainly the school's administration wanted a continuation of its basketball tradition, whatever their overall vision for enhancing the institution. Perhaps by that time, and under such conflicting pressures, Bo was feeling more than he was hearing. In any case, the residual affection for him never really waned, and he was always greeted warmly when later he'd return, whenever he could, to Hawk Hill. A basketball "lifer," Bo went on to help coach the Denver Nuggets in the NBA, under Paul Westhead, and also coached internationally. His new passion was golf, but his enduring passion remained his family.

When I finally took on the job he'd held for those nine eventful years, Bo and I continued to talk over the phone almost every day. The discussion would invariably gravitate to recruiting and players. Remembered as a great teammate by everyone who joined him on the court, Bo "saw" the game in the context of players' abilities and liabilities, but most of all their potential. He always had a word of advice and encouragement. The lesson that a college team is built by its players resonates in my ears every day, along with memories of Bo, although I never quite learned the intricacies of chess or Chinese.

The fourth and final goal of my career master plan had been to become the head coach of a Division I college program by the age of thirty-five, but I knew that I wasn't yet ready in any shape or form to take over the reins at Saint Joseph's. I'd already made that premature mistake at Bishop Kenrick. I did, however, want to stay on as an assistant, continuing to listen, learn, and hopefully expand my responsibilities.

It was loyalty, pure and simple, that had brought John Griffin back to Saint Joseph's in 1987 as a part-time assistant to Jim Boyle. Boyle had been a player here during the early years of the Ramsay era. Griffin had played during the less glorious years of Harry Booth. Booth, a fine athlete who captained and then coached both basketball and baseball, had succeeded the very successful Jack McKinney, but did not enjoy quite the same success on the hardwood. Perhaps some of Boyle's problems near the end of his tenure stemmed from having been a part of the glory days, and Griffin's more realistic approach from not having had that experience.

John Griffin, a coach straight out of Central Casting, with leading-man looks almost like those of Villanova's Jay Wright today, brought a business perspective to everything he did. He was probably the right man at the right time to right the ship. This can be a cyclical business. After graduation, he had been an assistant under Jim Lynam, the imaginative coach whose "four to score" scheme led to a remarkable turnaround in his three years following Booth. Griffin worked briefly under Boyle. He then became head coach at Siena College for four seasons, compiling a 70-44 record. Boyle had many outside interests. Griffin focused on only one. He was fascinated by finance, and left to make his career on Wall Street. Those eclectic interests of Boyle's gave him momentary release from the pressures of coaching. With Griffin's driven nature, the business at hand— whether bulls, bears, or basketball—was all-consuming.

When Griffin came back, initially to help Boyle, he may have sacrificed millions. I never really asked him about it. It may be that being the head coach at Saint Joseph's was the one job John

Griffin really wanted. It must have been for him to have given up so much. But when Griffin came back, it was for a love of the school no less than Boyle's. Character comes in many guises. As with Bo, I tried to study everything John did. In all the deep conversations I had with him, and most conversations with John Griffin tended to be deep, I never directly asked him one simple question about being head coach—did you enjoy it?

Griffin certainly brought in a business perspective that we didn't have before—and may not have too much now. I often say about our program that its greatest strength is that we don't do business, we do passion. Our greatest weakness is also that we don't do business. To this day I'm not quite certain what our overall budget is, and how much revenue we bring into the university. Based on what I've been reading, the former is minuscule compared to other Division I schools, and the latter, to the extent it can be measured, is immense. I certainly hope so. Maybe I should consult our excellent Haub School of Business, although we seem to be doing pretty well. However, I don't know that our program would be, even today, the kind of case study they'd want to use.

I can go just about anywhere on this campus and sit down and talk with anyone about how things are going. We have remarkable people helping me, but are we doing the very best job we can? In the rush of events, there's sometimes a lack of questioning. How can we do it better, and more efficiently? What are the long-term strategies? Well, I try.

What John Griffin found in 1990 was certainly not yet a catastrophe, but an evident decline—more a recession than a depression. But life, like business, isn't static—you're either progressing or regressing. For whatever reasons, we weren't bringing in the quality of player we had in the past. They were quality human beings, all right, and most of them graduated—an important measure of success in an educational institution. But we just weren't winning with them, and weren't likely to unless our level of recruits was raised in terms of their basketball quotient.

I like to think I helped in recruiting a winning kind of player, but we were all motivated by trying to duplicate John Griffin's drive. By 1993, Saint Joseph's was back in the postseason, playing in the NIT, and winning eighteen games. We had some great people who were also great players, like Mark Bass, Bernard Blunt, and Rap Curry. Griffin's unquenchable energy was encompassed by a mindset that never changed, whether we won or lost. But did he take time to enjoy it? I don't mean merely with an occasional smile or a laugh, but keeping it all in perspective. I think the image the public saw was the real John Griffin—driven and intense. That's the way he was every day. To his credit, he was smart enough to take breaks to make time to breathe. He'd leave his office around eleven o'clock some mornings and not come back until one-thirty or two in the afternoon. I don't think it was to take a siesta, and not likely to study Chinese or play chess.

I believe John was monitoring his investments, not just to make more money but to pursue his other consuming interest. It doesn't sound much like recreation, but he'd come back in the afternoon at least momentarily reinvigorated, after this interlude in his twelve-hour days. That degree of commitment was shared by everyone on his staff, none more than his devoted secretary, Clare Ariano. Working with and for John Griffin was exhilarating as well as exhausting, but I think eventually his own nature, in the context of coaching in so public an arena, left him emotionally drained.

However, just as Jim Boyle could laugh with anyone, John Griffin could talk with anyone. He talked with members of the board and repeatedly with Don DiJulia, as sensitive a director of athletics as any university ever had. Like Boyle, Griffin too strove for excellence, but his overall record was never quite satisfying enough for him: 75-69 in five years. He wasn't Jack Ramsay. His players never turned on him, any more than Bo's players had turned on him in harder times. But all that effort should have led to better results. We often talked about it. John couldn't turn off the criticism, any more than he could simply turn on more success. For once, he was distracted. He knew he was rebuilding a successful program we all sought, but it would take more time. There were debilitating injuries to players. There were setbacks. It couldn't be done overnight through the sheer force of John Griffin's will. I was close enough to him to understand. He had to be fully committed to whatever he did. He had reached the point, the tank empty, where he just couldn't go on. So he went to Don DiJulia and resigned.

I felt ready now, after ten years as an assistant coach, under these two very different but equally inspiring mentors. I was six years beyond the timeline of my own career path. We see things differently after forty than at thirty-five—or thirteen, for that matter. St. Joe's had been the team I rooted for as a kid, the ultimate goal I set for my coaching career. When a coaching change brought me the chance to finally climb up here as an assistant, it seemed more like Heavenly than Hawk Hill. But after you reach thirty-five, when you look around and see all those younger guys getting head-coaching jobs, and the same people from the same programs recurring over and over again, you begin to think it's never going to happen to you, that you'll become one of those career assistant coaches. There are so few opportunities, only some 336 head-coaching jobs in all of Division I men's basketball.

I knew we were rebuilding a great program here. It wasn't like I was looking at every opening. But when the job at Loyola College of Maryland came open, I viewed it as a place very much like Saint Joseph's. They would understand my values, where I'm coming from. I didn't want to uproot my family, but Baltimore is only a hundred miles from home. And so I applied and went down there for an interview. I went in fully prepared. As

Bo would note, even how you carry yourself can be important. Look people straight in the eye. Honestly, I thought I'd done a really good job and left feeling pretty confident. Apparently, word of the interview had gotten out. Three people—a couple of reporters and a friend—called to congratulate me. In some way they must have heard I was about to be hired. Unfortunately, they didn't tell Loyola's athletic director.

I may have left Loyola thinking that they liked the look in my eye, that I'd won the interview, but I didn't win the job. Of course, I never found out why. Deeply disappointed, I went out for a ride. When I returned, I found that note from my kids on the pillow, "Dear Dad, it's OK that you didn't get the job . . . . You will always be the best dad for us. You're number one in our hearts, and we love you very much." Any tears turned to pride. At least Judy and I had done something very right, more important than any job. I still look at that framed note very often in my office. It was the first thing I put there.

As discussed in the next chapter, applying for a job is not unlike recruiting a player. There are two acceptable answers in recruiting—yes or no. Being a second choice means nothing. I'm looking for a good fit, for both the prospect and the school. This isn't football. We've only thirteen scholarships to award. Two or three in the same year to the right student-athletes can make a great team and sustain a program. I went to that singular job interview very comfortable with who I was, looking for the right fit. But the fact is, in the back of my mind, if I had to put my hand on a Bible, I was probably looking for an avenue where I would end up back in Philadelphia. If you look around objectively, however, similar job opportunities here are few. When might one open up? Even with six Division I programs, by and large our local head coaches tend to stay a very long time.

Of course, there would be an opening, only fifteen months later, right down the hall. The Lord works in mysterious ways.

When John Griffin told me in July 1995 that he had resigned, he was good enough to add that he would recommend me as his replacement. And I honestly believed that I was the best person for the job, for that group of players at that particular time. However, I'd already learned that confidence in your qualifications doesn't necessarily translate to success. I soon knew precisely who I would be competing against. He was and is not only a friend of mine but a guy I had coached, James "Bruiser" Flint. He had said publicly that he really wanted this opportunity, acknowledging that it was an unusual pronouncement. But it came off well, representing his candor. If I'm sometimes compared to an unmade bed, the dapper Bruiser, now the head coach at Drexel, is more like the immaculate dresser in the middle of the room.

Moreover, Flint was a Saint Joseph's graduate, important to a program and an institution so rich in tradition. I didn't really fit the mold. Colleges were looking for young, dynamic guys who could really relate to the players, and someone with a solid track record as a recruiter. But I knew enough in my heart to believe, taking everything into account, that I was the best choice, and I was bold enough to tell that to anyone who would listen. In whatever field, if you don't honestly believe that, you might want to wait for a different opportunity.

I came to view this job, after the Loyola disappointment, as my one real shot. Even if I had to pursue others further afield, I wasn't cut from the cookie-cutter pattern most athletic directors seemed to be looking for, and I didn't want to travel all over the country like an itinerant salesman. This was it. Again, I prepared as thoroughly as I could, only more so. Of course, in many ways I'd already been prepared by Jim Boyle and John Griffin. I put together a checklist of things to do, and people I had to call. I spent a week doing all the things I thought were important in preparing to be a head coach, including a 100-day plan of what I'd try to do if I got it. Everyone who takes on a responsible new job should put together a 100-day plan. After all, the incoming president of the United States does it. And it will matter, because first impressions tend to be lasting.

My plan included everything from meeting with student leaders to organizing my staff, deciding who to retain and who to hire, reaching out to the faculty and former players, the alumni, every constituency of the university. Yes, I'd had contact with many of them over a decade, but it's different when you move over to a more autonomous position. Hopefully, there will be a honeymoon period, but it's not long. In the end, production will be more important than personality. You have to know precisely what you want to do—and hit the ground running—or you can be overwhelmed. But first, of course, you have to get the job.

I spent the week prior to my interviews trying to keep my ear to the ground, yet filtering out a lot of what I heard. Everyone had an opinion as to who should be the new coach, even what the hiring process should be like. I tried to focus on the positive. The ultimate interview was with Father Rashford himself, the esteemed president of the university. I had a private meeting with him. He'd known me peripherally as an assistant coach, but not really very well. Shaking or not, I wasn't about to be inhibited now. When he asked me, "What do you think I want?" I responded, "I think you want to hire me, but you don't know if you can. And that's my responsibility, to explain to you why you can and why you should." Which I proceeded to try to do.

The day I knew the decision was going to be made, I came to the office as usual, and time quite literally seemed to stand still. There is no tension like waiting for something important to happen over which you have no control. I had very much in my mind not wanting to disappoint my wife and children again, however gracefully they had accepted it before. The waiting was beginning to get to me. I left my office and started to drive aimlessly. As previously noted, I have little sense of direction. Somehow I wound up at Valley Forge Park. I got out and started reading the *Philadelphia Daily News* (with an eye to their sports section), sitting on a bench by a picnic table under a tree in that beautiful setting. I'd had the sense to remember to bring my cell phone with me. Fortunately, they were a lot bigger then. Late that afternoon the call finally came from Don DiJulia. He said the president of the university would like to speak to me. Father Rashford came on the line. "Phil, you're our man," he said. And I broke down.

When I called Judy, who had been saying the rosary, I tried to calm down and be clever, asking her if she had anything nice to wear to a press conference. Then we both cried, more or less together. I tried to find my way home. We lived in Drexel Hill at the time. I wanted very much to get there and tell my three children face to face. In his last public appearance before dying of cancer, Jim Valvano said that a day was not complete unless one both laughed and cried. That was a complete day.

Later I was asked to return to the campus, only a few miles from our home. Father Rashford wanted to extend the offer personally, a much-appreciated gesture. Then I met with some of the people in the athletic office and with the returning players, who were already set up for a meeting that day. I like to think they were all pleased. Characteristically, Bruiser Flint was most gracious, as well. Traveling home again to spend time with my family, I wondered how many miles I put on the car that day, but at least I knew I could afford the gas.

I had already written out what I wanted to say at the press conference. The message I wanted to impart was only finalized during this ten-day period. In essence, it had been composed years before. As I think about it now, it's not unlike the underlying theme of this book. We all make mistakes, but I wanted people always to be proud of how I represented my family name. I wanted them to be proud of the way I would represent the basketball program here, and everyone who had been a part of it. And I wanted them always to be proud of this university, the ultimate aim of our efforts.

I also knew who I wanted to invite. Enduring friendships are as rare as hidden treasure. Once you find them, they have to be cherished. Along with neighborhood friends and family, I have vivid recollections of everyone who went out of their way to be there, people I've long admired. Cathy Rush made time for the press conference. Geno Auriemma flew in from North Carolina, where he was recruiting. And there were so many others. As I said about Dwayne Lee, "Reach for a hand, touch a heart." Even to this moment, I can think of only five occasions the memories of which still bring me to tears—the day I was married, the birth of each of our children, and July 20, 1995. I was just thankful for the opportunity. I couldn't even recall the terms of my first contract—how much, for how long? Honestly, I had no idea, and as they say in Philly, I could care less. Honesty, however, impels me to add that I do know all these details of my employment today.

And then I started, armed with my checklist. It's even more important to me now. A careful checklist gives you a kind of comfort level: I have to do this today, this tomorrow, and this next week. Our most precious resource is our time. From the start I never really felt intimidated by this job, that it was beyond manageable dimensions. Confidence, however, is not the same as arrogance. I didn't sit back and say, "OK, now that I've achieved what I'd dreamed about for so long, I've got it made." For one thing, my record would in a matter of months be public knowledge. Fair or not, those victories and defeats would be mine to read about every morning, and equally available for others to judge.

Not everyone's job is quite so visible. However, I came prepared with the tools to do my best, and I would have the help of so many good people. In whatever profession, every day you either get better or you get worse. In terms of basketball, you may never be a great shooter (I wasn't), but you can always learn to play better defensively—and to become a better teammate.

As a businessperson, a coach, a teacher, even as a son or daughter, there's no such thing as staying the same. I believe wholeheartedly that each day we either improve or we decline. Life is all about competing, and often the competition is most of all against yourself. So you have to want to improve. And that is what I set out to do. If I can get even a little bit better each day, the program I administer will get better. The people around me will get better. As Princeton's innovative Pete Carril put it, "The measure of any teacher, provided he's not an egomaniac, is to see anybody that he taught do better than he did." And so, hopefully, over time, what we do together will help make our school better. In my thirteenth season as head coach, that goal remains the same.

CHAPTER 6

Teamwork's More Important than Talent

O F COURSE, WHAT COACH WOULDN'T WANT BOTH? It all came together for us, talent plus teamwork, in that memorable season of 2003–04. But talent without teamwork rarely leads to success. On the other hand, there are times, heartening to any coach, when teamwork will bring out talent. That happened to us the very next season, 2004–05, remarkable in its own right, when the whole became greater than the sum of its parts. In evaluating a talented recruit, the first thing I try to consider is what kind of teammate he is likely to make—or, as I put it in the previous chapter, will he be a good fit into our program? One indication is how he interacts with his family, his first team. Another is the observation of his coaches. But, as in all human relationships, projecting the future is an inexact process. The chemistry that connects people so that they will work as one is a rare mix. We're always looking for it, like scientists, and then trying to bottle it.

A coach can enjoy no greater satisfaction than when his best player also sets the standard for teamwork. Jameer Nelson, in my view the finest all-around player in the whole storied history of Saint Joseph's men's basketball, couldn't have put it better than after that wrenching loss to Oklahoma State in 2004 that kept us out of the Final Four: "My only goal was to be the best teammate anybody ever had." We ought to put that on the wall so everyone sees it as they enter our renovated fieldhouse, just as inside Penn's Palestra it says,

> TO PLAY THE GAME IS GREAT . . .
> TO WIN THE GAME IS GREATER . . .
> BUT TO LOVE THE GAME IS THE GREATEST OF ALL . . . .

I was thinking of titling one chapter of this book "Jameer and the Miracles," but there's nothing miraculous about such a season's success. It's true that there is bound to be some luck involved, games when everything just seems to come together, like the planets aligning, talent and teamwork meshing as one. But it all has to be based on substance from the start. I've read that, in these times of greater parity, even the best coaches in the best-funded programs may be fortunate to vie for the national championship more than twice in their entire careers. I don't buy it. It may be that 2003–04 was our dream season, the closest we'll come to the Holy Grail while I'm still around, but to be successful in this business you have to keep on dreaming.

Well, there I was in 1995, at least envisioning such success, in my modest office within our already venerable Alumni Memorial Fieldhouse, a newly minted head basketball coach. Yes, I'd brought in my plan of priorities with me, and hoped to hit the ground running. My first hundred days might not be so dramatic as, say, Franklin Roosevelt's in 1933, but I was hardly lacking in confidence. But there was also some inevitable anxiety. Imagine yourself, even as a highly valued clerk in a business, suddenly made office manager, or a salesman in the field called back to the main office to become director of sales, or an army sergeant on the battlefield elevated by events to second lieutenant—well, you get the picture. It's challenging enough just going to a new job, let alone supervising those you'd previously worked with as equals at the same old site—or, in my case, the same school. How do you relate to them? How do they relate to you?

When, seventeen years before, going to Bishop Kenrick, I sought the advice of all sorts of people, much of it was so contradictory that it was not easy to sort out. In preparing for this new responsibility, I'd done pretty much the same thing—but, with more experience, I could selectively make better use of it. Now was the time to turn specifically to those who had surmounted the same challenges I faced.

The first was my old friend Fran Dunphy. I spent an entire day with him. He had been an assistant coach at the University of Pennsylvania, although for only one season, before being named their head coach. (Today he's in the same capacity at Temple, coaching against players he'd recruited at Penn.) Fran's team and mine would soon be facing each other on the court, but it's a tribute to the fraternity of coaches, nowhere more than within Philly's Big 5, that he was so forthcoming and helpful to me.

Then I talked with Stan Van Gundy at Wisconsin, and several other coaches who'd had similar experiences. I had a lot of questions. I wanted especially to anticipate the possible pitfalls. In retrospect, what might you have done differently? What constituencies at your school are most influential? How do you allocate your time? What do you most regret? What happened that you didn't anticipate? What are your priorities now? I would only have this one opportunity to be a first-year head coach on the college level. It's no secret that I like to talk, but during this time, to my benefit, I did a lot more listening.

I also learned from high-profile people, in and out of coaching, from Pat Croce to Geno Auriemma, how they made time to fit in as many charitable and community activities as possible. Since there hadn't been a football team at St. Joe's for over half a century, media focus had long fallen even more on our basketball program. From the time I coached those kids' teams, I always wanted to give something back. Now I'd have opportunities beyond anything I could have imagined before to help make a difference throughout the area, from promoting programs that aid disadvantaged kids to raising funds to fight cancer.

But first my home base had to be secured, the source of any positive influence I might build in the wider community. Everyone who cared about Saint Joseph's had to know that their new head coach was as committed to academics as to success on the court. Our program had to maintain its positive image while winning more consistently. I owed that to every former player and coach, especially Jim Boyle and John Griffin, who had put me here. Without their support I would never even have been considered for this job. Just as with my family, I wanted to make them proud.

After absorbing so much advice, I vowed to be more visible, and vocal, giving the program a distinctive voice and working more directly with the media. There are a lot of other teams in this town. It wouldn't hurt the program or the school if I became known as something of a character. I've always been interested in semantics. Even in giving instructions, I think it is important to talk *with* people, more than simply at or to them. You will also get more productive input, helping everybody to use their time more effectively. From the start, I inherited a key asset, enabling me to put more into every day. Her name is Clare Ariano. She had served as the men's basketball secretary here since 1984. In 2005, she was inducted into our Hall of Fame. No one, player or coach, deserves it more.

I felt that Clare had been underutilized. Coming into our compact quarters just off the court, hers is the first face you see and the first voice you hear, our always-cordial official greeter to everyone who visits the basketball offices. From the start, Clare kept my very detailed weekly calendars. She probably still has some from that first year. Whenever there's a request for my time, I think it's important to find a way to say yes. "No" is not a major part of my vocabulary, as you would see by looking at all those calendars.

Often people ask me how I manage to do it, since I seem to be almost everywhere, from making pro football predictions on radio early in the morning to presiding over a silent auction (as silent as I can get) late that night. They should ask instead, "How does Clare do it?" Sometimes I'm not so sure myself, with all the things that go flying through and around and off and onto her desk. I understand there's an intercom between my office and her cubicle, but I rarely use it. Generally, I just yell over to her, mainly about where I'm supposed to be and how soon, and she yells back, or more often just comes in. Unlike me, she doesn't need a gym to stay slim. I'm not sure what we'll do when we move into those far more spacious facilities that are to come. Maybe I'll get a megaphone.

Clare's not only our greeter, she's my gatekeeper. The door to my office is almost always open, as I think it should be. If it's closed, Clare knows there's a reason, and it takes something of real urgency to interrupt. I haven't counted the total number of times, but I suspect the word "passion" may be used in this book more often than in a romance novel.

Every successful organization has a Clare. What we share most, I think, is that neither of us really feels that we're coming to work here each day. With all its demands, we love what we do. It's our passion. Like worker bees, I suppose, we couldn't live without it. The difference, of course, is that I get to be kind of the queen bee. I have all the opportunities to do things and meet people. I'm the public face of this program, and I'm very well compensated for what I do. Those who make it possible are the real heroes. "Thank you" is the most important and underused expression in the English language. No one has more reason to say it than I do.

This extends to my assistant coaches, gathered together in a similarly snug office (as things are now), adjacent to mine, not unlike graduate students might be, or seminarians. In a way, that's not a bad analogy. What we want the entire program to do is to enable young people to grow. I hope we help our players grow in every way, certainly in their skills, but more importantly into responsible adults. And if I'm helping to foster growth, I wouldn't want an assistant coach who didn't have the same ultimate ambition I did, to become a head coach. When I see Monté Ross, who was here for nine seasons (and is even more dapper than Bruiser Flint), leading the University of Delaware team today, or Matt Brady, who was here for eleven seasons, now head coach at Marist College, I feel the same kind of parental pride I hope Jim Boyle and John Griffin felt for me.

Staffing was probably the greatest challenge I faced at the outset, in 1995. It's a daunting task for anyone who becomes a leader, especially in his old workplace, requiring a lot of thought as well as some tact—not exactly my specialty. I had two friends who became convinced that I was committed to give them a job. It may well be that in casual conversations I had given them that impression. I still feel bad about it. One of those friendships has never been repaired, and the other took a long time to restore. On the other hand, I wanted Geoff Arnold, already an assistant coach I knew well, to stay on. He was a hard worker, a man of character, and completely committed to the program. Matt Brady I didn't know as well, but he had played for John Griffin, who spoke highly of him. For our third assistant coaching position, we brought back Carlin Warley, a former player.

I know it's only a matter of time before Mark Bass, my valued assistant for eight seasons who also played on my first team after I became head coach, will take the reins at another institution. He's too good not to. My other assistant coaches today are both starting their second seasons at St. Joe's—Dave Duda, who's already been a head coach at Delaware Valley College and at Widener and had played for me back at Bishop Kenrick, and Doug Overton, the standout player at La Salle University (and in the NBA), who I used to root against. As I've said, what a small world basketball is.

In whatever capacity, no one works *for* me. I want them to know that they work *with* me. We all work together for one employer, Saint Joseph's University. I don't want to come off as smug or self-indulgent. This book may be about me, but it only has value if it relates to *you*. It can only do that if I'm completely honest. As I said at the outset, I'm an ordinary guy with an extraordinary job. It's my experience in that job that provides a basis for giving people advice. This book is my conversation with you. I make mistakes every day, but I believe in the power of semantics and straight talk, and of walking the walk. There's no substitute for that in any aspect of life, even though it can be a lot easier to spell out than to carry out.

If my assistants' hands are going to get dirty, then my hands are going to get dirty, too. And if it's time to put up baskets for our summer camp, then I'm going to put up baskets with them. If there's a phone call from a kid at two o'clock in the morning, I hope it comes to me. You get a lot of such calls in coaching, and not only about basketball. Every college student has an official advisor, but as coaches we see these kids so much that the first call in an emergency may well come to us instead. I don't believe any leader can be above the day-to-day workers who report to him.

Some people may feel that a head coach hasn't the time to invest in mundane matters. We're supposed to be visionaries. That's what leads high-profile football coaches to view things from platforms in the sky, or high-profile basketball coaches to have limited access to their offices. I don't see that, and not solely because of lack of space. If you'll bear with a few bromides, slow and steady gets it done. Just make time. If you can go shoulder to shoulder, back to back, with the people who work with you, then whether they're your assistant coaches or secretaries or public relations people or staff, you're going to get a little bit extra from them. Selfishly, it will probably save *you* time in the end.

If people feel that you understand, then that makes you a more effective coach, a more effective leader, a more effective person. Because at the end of the day, that's what this is—a people business. It's not an X-and-O business. It's not a sneaker-contract business. It's not a television-show business. It's only about people. It's a person trying to connect with another person, on a one-to-one basis, fourteen times with the team, expanding to over four thousand times with our undergraduates, and beyond to our overall community and fans. If I can reach them, it's infinitely more important than the ability to draw up a play, although I like to think I'm pretty good at doing that, too.

My responsibility to my assistant coaches is most of all to have them ready, to be prepared to seize their opportunity when it comes. It might only come once, as I felt it did for me. Fortunately, what will most help them is also helpful for me. What they do daily, as I do, is coach players on the floor, teaching basketball. They recruit. They scout. They do public relations. They do community service. They are interacting with other departments throughout the university. We're not operating a closed corporation here, or a fiefdom. We're an interactive partnership. So you see, when another university comes calling on any of my assistants and asks not only, "Do you teach basketball?" but about any of these other areas, they can respond honestly, "Yes, I've done that, too."

Do I operate differently than other head coaches? If I do, I'm not saying it's better. I just know it's most comfortable for me, and my personality. I think the biggest mistake we make as people is that we let our titles dictate who we are. That's what you *do*, not who you *are*. And your titles can change. Right now, I hope I'm an author. Later today, I'll go back to being a coach. Tonight I may be an emcee at a charity function. I make over a hundred public appearances a year. But that's what I do, not who I am. I believe I was given a double gift at the Prep—the ability to write a coherent sentence and to speak in public. I've never been shy about that. I do still get nervous sometimes, if not really anxious about it. I think that will happen to anyone who cares about doing a job well. Whatever you do goes into making the person you are—not the title you carry.

When I reflect about the values of teamwork, my thoughts return to my very first team here as head coach. You may remember in *Goodbye, Mr. Chips*, that English schoolmaster, who when asked if he regretted not having had any children, replied that in fact he'd had hundreds of children, seeing in his mind's eye all of his former students over the years. Judy and I are blessed to have three wonderful children, but any teacher is bound to recall his past students. That first team I had, in 1995–96, was special, not only because they won nineteen games and went all the way to the NIT finals (where we lost to Nebraska, 60-56—what else is new?), but because of the distinctive young men who played on it. I think particularly about the seniors, whom I'd recruited as an assistant coach.

Since I've already cited an example of perseverance, I'd say Mark Bass defines leadership. I'm fortunate to have him still with me, at least for a while longer. He had been told his whole life that he was too small, that he'd never make it in basketball. That simply motivated him to try harder. All he did was come here, become a two-year captain, score over 1,000 points in his career (1,205, to be exact), play professionally, and is now on track in his coaching career. He was and is a very vocal leader, and a great teammate. Any coach would want a team of people like Mark Bass.

Then there was Reggie Townsend, an example of not being overly influenced by appearances. He never looked much like a basketball player, sometimes a little overweight, sometimes a lot. But could he score—the same averages as Bass during his senior season, and 1,246 points for his career. Reggie played a little bit of basketball in Europe, and then we lost contact with him. We've tried in vain to reach him. He, too, belongs in our Hall of Fame. But he doesn't return our calls. There are days when I wonder why. What did I miss there? What did I fail to see or do? Any teacher has such regrets. It hurts a little bit, even now.

Will Johnson was also on that team. He was a guy who was not serious at all about school or about basketball, for that matter. Why did he stick it out? Somehow he stayed eligible. John Griffin had tried to motivate him earlier, and I was very specific about his role on the team, our inside presence. Suddenly he flourished. All he did in his remarkable senior season was lead the entire Atlantic 10 in rebounding. We were able to squeeze a magnificent season out of Will, and now he's playing professionally in Europe.

It may be that the most extraordinary story of all those seniors on the 1995–96 team was that of Bernard Jones. On the surface, it's a hard-luck story. He had been here for five years. During that time he had endured two knee operations, and hadn't played in two years. But he was ready to play in what was in effect his senior season. My first game as head coach was at the University of Delaware, and the team won, 64-56. We came home to play Bucknell four nights later. I didn't tell anyone, but I started Bernard, his first game in two years. He got a standing ovation, and hopefully a memory he will never forget. Ten days later, he tore up his knee for a third time, and never played again.

At our team banquet, it was impossible to pick a single most valuable player. MVP awards were given to Will Johnson, Mark Bass, and Reggie Townsend. Reggie asked if he could say a few words. He told the audience that he was giving his award to Bernard Jones because Bernard had taught him how to be a man. It brought everyone to tears. If you touch people in whatever you do, in the deepest part of their being, then you're doing a good thing. I've been fortunate enough to have had many such memories since, but that first team was truly bigger than the sum of its parts.

How do we build such a team? First—and it can't be stressed too often—this is a people business. Despite some pitfalls, I learned this, too, in high-school coaching. A person is going to have good days and bad days. There are ups and downs, often for reasons I don't really know about. People have pride. They want to be proud of how they look and how they perform, to have gratification for the work they've done. So how do you tell the tenth man on your team, "You worked really hard, but you're not getting into the game"? That's the hardest thing I have to do. They all have dreams, and since we never stay the same in this life, I'm either propelling their dream forward or holding it back.

Just as every assistant coach should aim to be a head coach someday, every player who comes through our door probably feels he's destined to go to the NBA. The difference is that the odds favor our coaches. So when I tell a guy he's not going to play or he's not in the rotation, it's personal, even though I don't mean it personally. I'm crushing his dream. How do I make that up to him, and convince him that even in practice he's making a significant contribution to the team?

To me it's never been about a system. It's about building on foundations. It's absolutely essential that our players be willing to compete. That's the first pillar. We set up a competitive atmosphere throughout—in practice, in our scheduling, and our game opportunities. Yet, it's also essential to learn to share the basketball. To me, sharing the ball is the ultimate sign of respect on the court. That's the second pillar in building a team. I think it's really important that you take your shot, the third pillar. Everyone worked hard to get you that opportunity, and if you don't take it, that's worse than taking a bad shot. It sounds ironic, but teamwork is based on competition. To relate that to the wider world of work, suppose someone has prepared you for a promotion, to take a position in your company, and you decline to accept it. Your not taking the shot others set up for you is harmful to the whole organization. They thought you were ready, and put their effort behind you. You let them down, as well as yourself.

The fourth thing we ask of every player is to know your abilities, the key final pillar that holds the structure up. There's nothing harder than being realistic about yourself, but we all have to do it. Go to your strengths, stay away from your weaknesses. We will try to analyze both, as we've seen them, practice after practice. We will explain both to you, and then plan around your strengths, in combination with those of your teammates. But then you have to do the rest. If life is a competition, stressing your strengths is the way to be a winner. I don't want to make basketball bigger than it is, but it's the same lesson you'll need later in life. You may have to compete for a spouse. If she's what you're really looking for—great looks, great personality, great everything—it's just possible you may have some competition.

I know it sounds simplistic—to compete, to share, to take your shot when it comes, to really know your strengths and weaknesses—but that's what builds a team. Nobody does it alone. Look into the stories of great statesmen, great generals, great entrepreneurs, great leaders in any field, and see how they achieved success. It won't be a waste of your time. We don't study our history enough, and not our sports history alone.

How do we recruit such a team? When your grandparents were young, they used to talk about the "three R's" of basic learning: reading, writing, and 'rithmetic. (I guess spelling didn't rank very high.) In my mind, the three legitimate "R's" of effective recruiting come under the heading of *relationships, resources*, and *responsibility*.

I have only thirteen scholarships to give out, probably never more than five in any given year (as, for example, with our 2006–07 team). If either we or the prospect we've targeted makes a mistake, we both can suffer. I've referred earlier to the importance of honesty in recruiting, on both sides, but after we've specifically settled on a young man, we're in his hands.

The ultimate decision to accept our offer may be his, but hopefully only after he has seriously considered all those questions that should go into making the right decision. Relationships are probably the most important of our three R's, and, again, a lot of it comes down to teamwork. If the prospect is interested, he will accept our invitation to come to our campus. We want to present things as realistically as possible. We're courting him, but it's not an all-court press. The NCAA does not permit his visit to be longer than 48 hours. He won't, of course, spend all that time with me. My current freshmen will tell him they see me an average of about two and a half hours a day. I stress being accessible, but some days they won't see me at all. I might be off recruiting in Florida. There's no motivation for us to present a false picture. We house prospective student-athletes on campus during their visits, so, as they say on MTV, it's the real world. They eat in our cafeteria, and meet as many students outside the program as possible, in a natural setting.

Still, the choice is a challenge, because a lot of it is based on conjecture. Each recruit needs to consider, after he's met our current players but can't really know them all that well: Do you think you might have a better relationship with teammates at some other school than you could have here? Do you think you would have a better relationship with other students, outside of basketball, at another school? I may bring the prospect here, but the deal gets closed by the other people around our campus with whom he interacts, however briefly. We want him to meet as many faculty and staff members as possible. On this relatively small campus, we tell everyone who visits, you're going to be very well known and widely recognized if you come here. Whether that's a good or bad thing depends largely on what you're looking for.

There's no place to hide at Saint Joseph's. You're going to have to learn to deal, hopefully, with a degree of adulation as well as responsibility. You'll have close relationships with a lot of people—not only teammates but also former players who might turn out to be a key to your future. You'll have a personal relationship with me, and that won't end after you leave. That is vital to stress in recruiting, but hard to prove in advance. There's nothing quantitative about it that he can touch. It's a quality the recruit has to accept on faith, and what he's heard from others. Every coach will probably tell him something similar. All I can say is that we mean it.

Resources are easier to grasp. Do we have what you need at this university to enable you to pursue your lifelong dream? That's not true if you consider only our basketball resources, although they will soon be upgraded. Yet to my knowledge we've never had a recruit go elsewhere for resources alone, and if he did, we'd probably have been better off without him. But more than bricks and mortar, are you going to get outstanding coaching? Are we going to play a high-quality schedule? Do we have what you need to come in and work on your game, a one-on-one emphasis? Do you find playing in the famed Palestra, having access to a great city, and the opportunity to travel, appealing prospects? (We don't get too many "no's" to that one.)

How about resources to help you prepare for your future, in or out of basketball? Do the Fortune 500 companies come to our campus? Do we have prominent alumni who can open the door for you? (Not automatically give you a job, but the opportunity to make your case.) Are the resources here to help you make friends for life? How easy is it to network, to widen your circle of friends? If you're from outside the area, is a new friend in your freshman dorm likely to take you home to dinner with his family?

Again, a lot of this is conjecture, or based on initial impressions, but isn't such interaction more likely at a smaller university? On the other hand, would you prefer all the options of a university with 20,000 students or more? Do you want to be on television every time you play, be the biggest story in town? Can we meet your academic goals? If your aim is to be a marine biologist, let's be honest; we just don't have those specific resources, and can't create them for you. Fortunately, not too many basketball players are intent on a career in marine biology.

Relationships, resources, and the third quality, responsibility. As outlined, I try to talk not only to a recruit's coaches but particularly to his parents. The first team is family. In these times it may not be the traditional pairing of mother and father. But whether parents, a single parent, mentors, or guardians, you're asking for the ultimate in responsibility—for them to give you their pride and joy. In most cases, they are handing him over into your care for four of the most important years in his life.

No one should take that responsibility lightly. Academically, socially, athletically—this has to be the right school for him. Whether their son comes here or not, I hope they will look back and say, "You told us the truth. You did it the right way." Whatever happens, we'll wind up with enough quality players to have a quality team, and hopefully they will all be good team-mates. Of course, we want talented players, but only if they're really happy here.

In the process of recruiting, there are only two answers, yes or no. It is just like recruiting a new employee. You want to hear yes or no as quickly as you can—in our peculiar circumstances, as soon as possible after a recruit makes his key visits to colleges. At that point, the answer "I don't yet know" will probably wind up wasting everyone's time. Think about it. Reduced to its simplest form: "Do you want to go out on a date?" "Do you want this job?" "Do you want to come to our school?" If the answer is "I don't know," the fact is, they probably *do* know, and so do you. It's just hard to say no. It's time for you to move on to someone else. "Do you want to get married, Judy?" Thankfully, she didn't reply, "Well, I'll think about it."

UNDOUBTEDLY THE HARDEST loss for most of our fans—and we gained so many new ones during that wonderful season of 2003–04—was, of course, our final game, the squeaker with Oklahoma State. The fact is, I thought our final game with Xavier in the Atlantic 10 championships of the 2005–06 season was tougher to take, at least for me. Our expectations were not so high. We lost by only one, 62 to 61, and ultimately went down in the second round of the NIT to Hofstra, in overtime, 77 to 75. But I understand how people felt when Jameer's final shot fell short, and we lost by two on March 27, 2004, keeping us from the Final Four. Still, imagine, a season of 30 and 2.

The day after that game, I went to Mass. I met three people leaving the church who rather tentatively came over to me. And before they could finish what they wanted to say, each of them broke down in tears. Those were adults, acquaintances rather than close friends, but the whole experience had moved them perhaps more than the outcome of a single basketball game should. Yes, it really hurt at the time, and it still lingers in memory. My family hurt, the staff hurt, our players hurt most of all, but so did those people at church, and probably people we'll never know watching on television around the nation. But, as I told my players, "If this is the worst day of your life, then you will have a very blessed life." However, as I reflected after that Sunday in church, what an accomplishment it is to have moved people's emotions like that.

We've enjoyed a lot of success, but our program has had so many similarly close calls. I hope I've learned something from each of them. As I say, you need the right temperament to stay in this business. After our undefeated regular season in 2003–04, how could we lose to Xavier by twenty points in that year's Atlantic 10 tournament? The onus was on me because I had not prepared my players for the desperation of a good team. And, of course, the target was on us, the number one team in the nation. I knew five minutes into that game that we were going to be severely challenged. I don't think you can do anything about yesterday, or two days from now. But I know you can do everything in your power about today. In sports, as in recovery, it's one day at a time.

Because we had pulled out so many games in so many different situations all season, twenty-seven in a row, I had been talking not about the next game, our immediate goal, but about the Atlantic 10 championship, three games out. We lost focus because I lost perspective. We weren't on task against Xavier. Our players, however stunned, had the satisfaction of knowing they had more games to play. We would still be a number-one seed in the NCAA tournament, the "Big Dance." However, to me, getting crushed by twenty can be more devastating than being nipped by two. Maybe that's why I seek solitude on game days.

The following season, to be inspired by the teamwork of a far less talented group, as they scratched and clawed their way to twenty-four wins and the final of the NIT, only to lose to South Carolina by three, was very tough to take, just as with those close calls that concluded our following season of over-achievement. All the way to the brink, and back. There's no finality more sudden than the end of a season, for many the end of a playing career. But consider all those experiences. Every one of these teams overachieved, whether the final tough loss was to Nebraska, Auburn, South Carolina, Hofstra, or Oklahoma State.

The point isn't what we got our players to do to reach such heights, or that we didn't make it all the way. In every season only one team makes it all the way. It's what they did together, more than anyone could have expected. Even that dream team of 2003–04 overachieved, in the mature way they dealt with the media, despite their insistent drumbeat of "Can you do this?" or the selfless way they played, and the way they handled both the adulation and the disappointment. What a message for young people everywhere. At the start of Dr. Jack Ramsay's book on winning basketball, he quotes his favorite poem, "If," by Rudyard Kipling, about triumph and disaster, and treating "those two imposters" just the same.

In fact, a number of the members of that 2003–04 team have realized their hoop dreams. Three are playing in the NBA today, and a fourth could possibly join them. Several are playing in Europe, and it appears that every one of them, including the walk-ons, is headed for a productive career. As the NCAA stresses, very few college athletes will "major" in sports after they graduate, so this talented team is a kind of aberration. But their teamwork set a standard for others, few of whose members are likely to play professionally. If their experiences at Saint Joseph's helped prepare them for fulfilling lives, isn't that what it's really about? We had them with us for significant seasons, learned from each other, and went on, mutually enriched.

Since I've already quoted the Bard of Avon, why not add something from "the Wizard of Westwood"? In his own book, *They Call Me Coach*, John Wooden also reprinted a poem, not from someone famous but by a teacher named Glennice L. Harmon. It expressed his own view, as it does mine today, "They ask me why I teach, And I reply, Where could I find more splendid company?" I guess we coaches just like poetry.

CHAPTER 7

Mid-Majors and Minor Matters

IT WAS QUITE A THRILL. The February 16, 2004, issue of *Sports Illustrated* arrived with a confident-looking Jameer Nelson on its cover, legs apart, one hand on his hip, the other holding a basketball, with that characteristic slight smile on his face. They really captured him, the Jameer we all knew.

The cover caption was

MEET
JAMEER NELSON
THE LITTLE MAN FROM THE LITTLE SCHOOL
THAT'S BEATING EVERYONE

The six-page article inside also included photos of Delonte West and Tyrone Barley, as well, and even one of me looking tense in a huddle ("Martelli showed the strain of a 20-0 start by chewing out a fan."), but I'm sure Jameer would have been happier had the featured two-page spread

FULL NELSON
Led by Jameer Nelson, the nation's best player, little St.
Joe's started 20-0 and is thinking big

pictured the entire team instead of his own mid-air leap to the basket, surrounded by Villanova players.

Although it was a flattering, perceptive article by Michael Bamberger, and by no means were we tiring of all the attention during that memorable (I'm running out of adjectives . . . "dream," "magical," "unforgettable," anything but "miraculous") season, I don't think I was alone in tiring a bit of the inevitable David vs. Goliath analogies. At that time, with only weeks to go, of all the programs in Division I men's college basketball, only Saint Joseph's and Stanford were still undefeated. "Can they run the table?" *SI* speculated, listing future opponents. I knew what was coming next. What a contrast: "Stanford has a gorgeous campus, a movie-star handsome senior guard and a coach with a regal bearing, suitable for Mount Rushmore. St. Joe's has a cramped campus that fronts suburban sprawl, a senior guard built like an 11th-grade fullback and a coach who looks like the guy down the street who gets his newspaper in his pajamas." (Didn't I tell you?)

That's how it went all season, the comparisons too tempting to overlook. That particular article continued along the same lines, noting Jameer's eight tattoos, our ancient "Erector set" of a gym, even quoting some "old school" Jesuit priests who supposedly proclaimed that "Saint Joseph's is a humble institution with much to be humble about." Did we, the Little Sisters of the Poor, really belong with the big boys? Still, how appealing, and, except for the modest size of our selective school, how utterly untrue. Had anyone read a recent college guide?

As our new president that year, Timothy R. Lannon, S.J. (who, no offense to Stanford's coach, Mike Montgomery, really does look more suitable for Mount Rushmore), put it at the time, "We've got a great program and a great university. In my mind Duke and Stanford are great company these days." Father Lannon had enjoyed fortuitous timing, coming from Marquette, whose men's basketball team during the preceding year had enjoyed a remarkable run of its own, all the way to the Final Four. You don't need football to stir things up with your student body.

Size may matter in some areas, but not in the quality of an academic institution nor in motivating the success of its athletic teams. For that matter, wasn't David a lot better-looking than Goliath? You didn't see Michelangelo or Donatello carving statues of Goliath. I wondered how many of those observers of the hoops scene had actually visited our campus. Compact it is, although it will soon get a lot larger, but hardly grim. At its leafy heart since 1927 has been magnificent Barbelin Hall, with its Gothic tower, carillon, and courtyard, not unlike those at Yale. For many years, until those new skyscrapers evoked "Billy Penn's curse," the top of that tower marked the highest point from sea level in the city of Philadelphia. Hawks were reportedly observed flying over it, before swooping down on their prey. That's why the site of Saint Joseph's University is still called Hawk Hill.

We Americans like to categorize things. As I've said, I'm fascinated by semantics. Although I use it all the time, including in this book, I'm not sure when "at the end of the day" became the accepted term for the conclusion of any period of time, or when the most lethal armaments became all but officially called "weapons of mass destruction" (or simply "WMDs"). Why all the extraneous words? Why "at this point in time" instead of simply "at this time"? What are "flu-like symptoms"? I don't even want to contemplate how a "sports hernia" differs from any other.

Nevertheless, at some point in time, somebody divided all those Division I basketball programs into "majors" and "mid-majors" (I'll bet there are also some "minor-majors" out there, like in the solar system), apparently based mainly on computerized conclusions like strength of schedule, and what conference you're in. A lot of the smaller, better academic colleges and universities in Division I seem to wind up as mid-majors. It has a significant impact on who gets into the NCAA tournament, and that bonanza for "bracketologists" has led to some universally accepted terminology of its own—"March Madness," "Sweet Sixteen," "Elite Eight," "Final Four."

Your school's chance of making it through all the way, involving winning six games, or even of becoming one of the sixty-five entrants at the start, can be influenced from the outset by whether you're from one of the "power" conferences— the Atlantic Coast Conference, the Big 10, the Southeastern Conference, the Pac 10, the Big East, the Big 12, and so on—or only a mid-major. The ACC may get six or seven of its schools into "the Big Dance"; the Patriot League, for example, only one—the champion of its own postseason tournament. Its regular-season champion, if a different school, now goes to the National Invitation Tournament. In fact, for the past four years, the number of "at large" bids for mid-major schools in the NCAA tournament has actually declined. All this has certainly affected us. It may be that our showing in 2003–04, and that of some other schools like Xavier, helped transition our Atlantic 10 Conference from mid-major to at least limited power status, increasing our opportunities.

I guess right now we're kind of in the middle—depending on their records and power rankings, generally two of our member schools have a solid chance to make it to the NCAA's, and one to the NIT. During the past four years, A-10 representation in the NCAA tournament has fluctuated between only one participant and the four schools that made it in 2003–04. After our 2006–07 regular season and A-10 tournament, it was two. Circumstances change every season.

Still, this whole pre-categorizing of institutions is ridiculous. Yes, a team from a power conference generally wins the national championship. Unless it's Duke, it will likely be some mega-sized public university. In 2006 and 2007, it was the University of Florida. But during every season's tournament there are "Cinderellas," most recently George Mason and Bucknell, from those mid-major conferences. How exciting! And every season there are near-upsets in the tournament by the top academic institutions in the nation. In 2006, Penn, champions of the Ivy League, which has no postseason tournament, nearly upset Texas. Elite little Davidson, with a student body of 1,700, nearly upset Ohio State. How inspiring!

During the past season, watching Holy Cross of the Patriot League play with mighty Duke of the ACC, I heard the announcer refer to a Holy Cross player as a "mid-major all-star." It appears that the separation has even come to that. Aren't we all created equal in this country, at least in opportunity? Of course, some of this success is based on greater parity. When I started coaching, even the most talented college players had graduation as their likely goal. Now so many, particularly from the big-time schools, go pro after only a year or two, it gives the less publicized programs more of a chance to compete with their predominantly four-year players.

I suppose, if this really matters enough for me to get worked up about it, it's because of how *we've* been perceived in the past. Even as we made that incredible run to the edge of the Final Four in 2004, there were still experienced observers who felt that we really didn't belong in the company of the giants, that we weren't worthy of our number-one seeding. Mind you, a Ramsay-led team had actually gone to the Final Four over forty years before.

What a proud tradition we represented. It's been twenty-two years since three Catholic universities—Villanova, Georgetown, and St. John's, all from the major Big East Conference—comprised three of the Final Four. With the more recent success of Gonzaga, Marquette, Xavier, and Saint Joseph's, who can define which school is or isn't a major contender, and why?

ALTHOUGH I DIDN'T make the cover of *Sports Illustrated*, my regal visage did grace the covers of other publications that season, such as *Coach and Athletic Director* (the one that doesn't have an annual swimsuit issue). They must have seen *HawkTalk*. I was featured as "Martelli the Magnificent" and "King of (Hawk) Hill." Not surprisingly, I was being interviewed far more than ever before, and the phone calls, correspondence, and e-mails multiplied exponentially (that is, quite a lot). I can only imagine the ticket requests that inundated Don DiJulia. It was a heady time.

In terms of my own emotions, I think Tom McGrath captured them pretty accurately in the March, 2004, issue of *Philadelphia Magazine*, contrasting my "wacky wisdom" with the "grim control freaks" he felt dominated big-time college sports. During a quiet interlude in my car, he sensed my concern that greater notoriety not change how I did or viewed things. He called it "the uneasy underbelly of success." Just because there were so many more of them, why shouldn't I continue to return calls promptly, to keep trying to connect with people, to still know their first names? Someone I admire once said, "Integrity is nothing more than showing the same face to everybody."

McGrath was kind enough to conclude that Phil Martelli is "determined to balance [his] intensely competitive nature—and don't be fooled by the goofiness, Martelli wants to win . . . but not at the cost of the principles his parents and the Jesuits at St. Joe's Prep instilled in him. Be polite. Work hard. Show respect. Stay true to your family and your roots, and above all, don't take yourself too seriously."

But I do take my job seriously, and my pride in the stature of this splendid school our teams represent. When, early in my tenure, a Hall of Fame coach, Lute Olson of the University of Arizona, cancelled an already-scheduled game with us without even informing me, I exploded. True enough, the winter weather here had been severe, making travel potentially hazardous, but why didn't he contact me first? He wasn't disrespecting Phil Martelli, he was disrespecting Saint Joseph's University. Our team, under John Griffin, had flown all the way out to Arizona to play them only a few years before. I'll never know, because Olson hadn't even the courtesy to call me. He simply announced the scheduling change to the press, as if that's all that was necessary. In my subsequent press conference, I denounced both his decision and his discourtesy as completely unacceptable. There was and is nothing personal about it. I've run into him since at coaches' meetings, but he does no more than nod. We've never talked it out, as I would like to have done.

Although I stress composure on the court, at least once I've blown up publicly at a fan—not a very good example for my players. The object of this rare epithet was a supporter of St. Bonaventure, and hardly one of the customary rowdies you see and hear on the road. In fact, as I later learned, she was a staid, middle-aged librarian, a respected educator who had once coached high-school basketball herself, and a season-ticket holder at the Bonnie's home games. Unfortunately, that enabled her to sit only a few rows behind our bench, so close she could listen to our huddles.

Normally, in my statesman's stance on the sidelines, hands either clasped behind me or across my chest, I've mentally conditioned myself to ignore all the epithets. I already know that I'm bald. And I've repeatedly told my players, as well, to focus between the lines, especially at away games where we're bound to be targeted, to be oblivious to the inevitable vocal abuse, and just play our game. Winning is the most effective response.

The problem was, on this chilly January night in 2004, in upstate New York, in what would be our seventeenth straight victory, our guys were playing almost too well. It's as if everything we had practiced was working nearly to perfection. We went on to win 114 to 63, the only time that season we would break 100. By halftime, frustrated fans of our opponents were yelling things like, "Quit pouring it on" and "Phil, you stink," among their more printable comments. By now we were used to it. However, scoring aside, what has upset me increasingly in recent years is the decline of civility in our sport, the increase in the kind of personal obscenities that discourage the female members of my family, for example, to attend away games. It isn't too far from "Air ball!" to "You suck!" and much worse. Sad to say, I think it reflects an overall coarsening of our society.

However, throughout that game I was thinking more of what an extraordinary exhibition of basketball we were witnessing. If you're a real fan of the game, whichever side you may favor, appreciate what you're seeing here. It's worthy of emulation, not denigration. Everything was working so well for our team, I don't know if I could have turned it off—it was near perfection. But after I kept hearing this lady behind our bench yell directly at me, "Why are you pressing with a 25-point lead?" I finally kind of lost it. I wheeled around and responded, "Shut up, you nitwit!" In a way, it felt good, for once, to yell back.

A young reporter nearby insists that I followed up by also calling her a "moron," but I don't recall any further comments. All I know is that in a subsequent press conference, he turned this brief verbal exchange into a much bigger deal than it was. The press picked it up. "Is the pressure getting to this whack-job Martelli?" What pressure? That game was a rout. The fact is, no matter what our record is in any given season, and however controlled my customary demeanor on the court, like most coaches, I feel some pressure before and during every game.

We have a tendency in this country to blame everything on "the media." Although I affirm, "If you can't stand the heat, stay out of the kitchen," I do believe that in this instance an ambitious young reporter managed to turn a minor incident into a major issue. Unaware of how widely it was being reported, I was surprised to get a call from Don DiJulia. His three-year interlude in a seminary must have been excellent preparation for dealing with the likes of a Phil Martelli.

DiJulia was our unsung hero throughout that season, coping with all the pressures and the praise—our godfather, the link between past and present (he had played both basketball and baseball at St. Joe's in the 1960s, and started the first of his two stints as athletic director in 1976), and was never far from a phone. That call from him came so soon after the game that I knew something was up. What was this business with a fan? It was all over the wires. Of course, it died down soon enough. I'd already decided to call the lady. Her name was in all the Sunday papers. First I Fed-Exed a personal letter to her, "Please accept this apology for my childish comments." Then I called her. At least we had a chance to talk it out. I never did get a call from Lute Olson.

Billy Packer is a different story. Whatever the resulting excesses of hype and hysteria, all of us in this business owe a tremendous debt of gratitude to the television personalities who have made the college game, and especially "March Madness," so incredibly popular—the Dick Vitales, Al McGuires, Bill Rafterys, and Billy Packers. I didn't realize in 2004 that Packer had been a pretty good player himself, a guard at Wake Forest, and had once played against Saint Joseph's. Although he'd not seen us that season, I imagined so perceptive an analyst should know our story pretty well. Even after finally losing that A-10 tournament game to Xavier, we were still 27 and 1. I knew we'd be a first or second seed in the NCAA tournament. There isn't a more thoroughly informed group in the nation, including congressional investigating committees, than the NCAA committee that carefully determines these seedings, and they decided we should be the number-one seed in the East.

Then Packer announced to the world that we just didn't belong up there with the real majors, those other top seeds. Though we'd undoubtedly played well on our own level, plucky little St. Joe's was simply not up to theirs. As I recall, some others may have made similar comments, if not with such disdain.

I was infuriated. Again, as with Lute Olson, it was nothing personal. I'd never met Packer. But he was disrespecting my team, whose whole body of work had been out there for everyone to see, as well as the stature of our school and the Atlantic 10 Conference itself. If he just didn't see us competing with the likes of the Atlantic Coast Conference, why not wait and see? Throwing a bucket of cold water on our parade now diminished everything our players had accomplished. Packer's style is not to rant or rave. It was not quite a tirade, just his premature observation. It might even serve as an incentive for us, but I saw it as an insult, pure and simple.

I've intended this book to be suitable for all ages. So you might want to exercise parental discretion and keep your kids from this page. My first reaction, after being called out in this way, was to blurt out, "Billy Packer can kiss my ass!" I'm sorry, but there it is. As luck would have it, we were progressing in the East Regional to a potential showdown with . . . Wake Forest. I did eventually get to see Packer, suggesting that I'd helped promote his career, and we both smiled. As I say, I've long admired his professional work and the thoroughness of his preparation, although I still question how much he really knew about us. While generally understated, he can be very opinionated. Since I imagine he felt he was just being honest, I don't think he ever fully understood why my reaction had been so vehement.

But before we got to take on Wake Forest in the Sweet Sixteen of the NCAA tournament in East Rutherford, New Jersey, we would have to get through two games in the first round in Buffalo, New York. As the top seed in the East, we got to play relatively close to home, but should we make it through to the Final Four, that would mean traveling to San Antonio. Fine with us.

In the first game we defeated Liberty University handily, 82 to 63, even with Jerry Falwell on their side. That meant facing Texas Tech, coached by the redoubtable Bobby Knight. However controversial, he is one of the giants of our profession, and I've always admired him. If he's brutally blunt and hard on his players, consider how well many of them seem to have done later in life. Most recently he was criticized for grabbing and pulling up a player's chin, insisting he look his coach directly in the eye. I might not have done it that way, but the fact is, looking people right in the eye is always a good idea. It can even help you land a job.

Before the game, Knight came up to me and complimented my team, commenting on how their example of no-nonsense team play was good for college basketball. Generally, coaches merely exchange pleasantries prior to a game, and this one was to advance to the Sweet Sixteen. I was impressed with his gesture. It was a predictably tough game, but we pulled it out 70 to 65. With five minutes to go, the game was tied, but then Pat Carroll hit a three, and Jameer Nelson did his thing.

Afterwards, even-tempered Jameer put it succinctly, "What are they going to say now? That our uniforms are ugly? It's a shame people want to knock us—for what reason? We're together. All we need is us." But the fact is, we were picking up a lot of new fans from all over the country, many of whom had never seen our team play before. Talent won't win without teamwork, a theme Knight echoed after the game. Saint Joseph's plays "unselfish and they play hard . . . . It's good for kids to see a really good team play like these kids do."

I was even more impressed by the comments of one of Knight's seniors, a kid—or perhaps I should say a *man*—named Michael Marshall. Imagine, he had just played the last game of his college career, our players were celebrating, and in the midst of it he came over and told me, "We take great pride in our toughness, and I want you to know your team is as tough as any team we've faced . . . in the heart. And because of that, everybody at Texas Tech will be pulling for you to win it all." How much does that say for the kind of people and the kind of programs Knight, today the winningest coach in Division I men's basketball, has overseen all these years?

It was on to New Jersey, and a meeting with the Demon Deacons (isn't that as much a contradiction in terms as the Fighting Quakers?) from a very fine university named Wake Forest. The venue is now called the Continental Airlines Arena, in the desolate Meadowlands. It had originally been named the Brendan Byrne Arena, for New Jersey's governor at the time. Fame is fleeting in this corporate era. There is a wonderful paperback book, nearly 100 pages, put out by our sports information people that tells the whole story of that special season as it unfolded, through vivid newspaper accounts. It's not remotely our intention to try to duplicate it here, but, of course, some games just stand out.

The very first that season, against tenth-ranked Gonzaga, which we won by seven, was an early indication that something exceptional might be in store. It was not only a perfect regular season, 27 and 0 for our team, but for Delonte West, there was also a perfect game. With the Hawks trailing by six against Xavier during the regular season in their tumultuous home court in Cincinnati, West went on a tear, shooting 12 for 12, making 6 for 6 from the foul line, plus six rebounds, five assists, and three steals—the epitome of a clutch performance, totaling 33 points. Then there was our two-point win at Rhode Island, an earlier three-point win against California, and a three-point win against Old Dominion. It's never easy to build such a record in any year.

There's nothing like the solidarity of Philly basketball. In the stands up in the Meadowlands was everybody from Pennsylvania governor and avid sports fan Ed Rendell, who went to Penn, to Bill Cosby, who all but personifies Temple. They weren't rooting for Wake Forest. At courtside, Billy Packer was also present, along with some 19,500 other spectators. The game was very close, to no one's surprise, except perhaps Packer's. Wake led at the half, 38 to 37. As with Texas Tech, we fell behind early. Then our threes began to fall. First, Tyrone Barley's, then Pat Carroll's, then Delonte's. Our lead fluctuated. Only poor foul-shooting kept it tight down the stretch. Wake went to a zone and got closer, but we ultimately won by four, 84 to 80. Between them, Nelson and West scored 48. Wake made 8 of 16 treys, but we countered with 12 of 24. Both teams shot well, but we were able to "build a wall," as one newspaper account put it, around Wake's star, Chris Paul, holding him to 12 points.

Before the game, as Dick Jerardi described it in the *Philadelphia Daily News*, from the balcony of our team's hotel, Father Lannon spoke directly to the players as well as some 1,000 Hawk faithful gathered in the lobby. "'Our promise to them is that we'll be right there tonight,' Lannon said, 'We'll be with them Saturday and we'll be with them in San Antonio.' With that, the band began to play and the team walked through the lobby to the bus. The same scene will play out tomorrow," Jerardi continued. "All we need to find out is what's next." I wonder how many other college presidents also said Mass for his school's fans.

Jerardi noted how it had all begun only four and a half months before, on November 14, 2003, but a few miles away in

New York's storied Madison Square Garden, when launching this "season of unforgettable moments," we had prevailed over Gonzaga. That was thirty victories ago.

Of course, my old friend "Hoops" Weiss, in the *New York Daily News*, put me in the middle of the story: "Martelli has hanky in hand." Ignoring the fact that my favorite TV program, even in reruns, is the decidedly unemotional *Seinfeld*, a "show about nothing," Weiss noted how I "got misty" at movies from *Rocky* and *Radio* to *Hoosiers* and *Seabiscuit*. The fact is, I *am* affected by such "sports flicks." They're all about underdogs. Later I'd love *Cinderella Man*, as well. As that guy said in *Seabiscuit*, "It's not the size of the horse that matters, it's the size of the heart in the horse." Weiss went on to write, "That's what has made this little Jesuit school on City Line Ave. such a compelling saga in this NCAA tournament, and such an endearing story down in gritty Philadelphia." OK. Now we're not only minuscule, but our beautiful city is "gritty." Did anyone mention that Wake Forest has only a few hundred more students than Saint Joseph's? You can only put five players on the floor at a time, even if your university is ten times larger. We were still seeded first in the region, ranked first in the nation.

The road to the Final Four went through second-seeded Oklahoma State, winners of the very major Big 12 Conference, and coached by the vastly experienced Eddie Sutton. They were favored by two and a half points, largely because of their tough inside play. We had six-foot-eleven Dwayne Jones to patrol the lane, but all season we had relied on our tenacious guard-based perimeter offense. All four of those guys could shoot, but would we be physical enough to prevail?

Well, you all know the story. Although out-rebounded almost two to one, and with no one shooting particularly well, we still led by six at the half. It would have been more had anyone matched his effort against Wake Forest. Delonte did eventually get to 20 points, but our team overall shot less than 39 percent for the game, although committing only five turnovers. The Cowboys warmed up in the second half. They took the lead; we'd take it back. It went down to the wire, eventually decided by three plays in the final minute.

Pat Carroll, our best long-distance shooter, had suffered through an uncommonly tough time, but all three of his successful field goals (out of eleven shots) were three-pointers. It looked as if the final one might seal it, giving us a 62 to 61 lead. However, with only some twenty seconds left, Pat left the man he was guarding, John Lucas III, to pursue a loose ball. An OSU teammate scooped it up and passed to Lucas, son of the former NBA star, who calmly sank a three-pointer. Jameer, with an opposing player in his face, rushed down the court with seven seconds left to go. With only a second left, he launched a prayer from 16 feet. It wasn't answered. We can all still see the picture in our minds. It clanged off the front of the rim. Final score: Oklahoma State 64, Saint Joseph's 62.

A more enduring image is that of Jameer sitting dejectedly on the floor, the winners celebrating nearby. In a reversal of the scene after our own victory over Texas Tech, several of Sutton's players came over to console Jameer, so high did he stand in their estimation. They'd been through a war together. As I said an hour after the game, "If you're gonna go out, go out like that . . . giving everything you have." John Feinstein put it well in the *Washington Post:* "The Hawks didn't die and neither did the dream. It just came up a few inches short."

USA Today estimated the millions our school made in increased ticket sales, gear, enhanced television revenue, and publicity essentially because Jameer decided to come back for his senior season, making a good team great. I prefer to focus on all the enduring good will, on which no price can be placed. Everyone knows who we are now. As I said at the time, it was the best story in America, and it *should* be celebrated. The amazing coast-to-coast press coverage we received was one of the great benefits of that season.

My favorite name for a sportswriter who covered us consistently is Tom Archdeacon of the *Dayton Daily News*, undoubtedly given to piety—even though he called me the "Philly Freak." He went on during that season to describe me further as "a guy with grandma's crumbs on his shirt, rosary beads in his pocket, and all of college basketball at his stocking feet." Ah, the glories of our free press—but it was quite a story.

It was teamwork plus talent. In my mind, there was something special about every player on that unselfish team, including the walk-ons. One of them, a gregarious senior from Sewell, New Jersey, named Rob Hartshorn, a memorable character who only got to play in blowouts, had some perceptive things to say about some of his teammates, as reported by Steve Serby of the *New York Post*.

Here is Rob's view from the bench. On Jameer Nelson: "He looks kinda like the old guy at the playground, [but] he can dominate whenever he wants to." Off the court: A great sense of humor, despite being seemingly so soft-spoken. "Once he pretended he forgot to bring my cheese-steak just to get to me. I found it in my locker, only it was two feet long, with a soda and my change lying underneath of it." On Delonte West: "I've never seen a more fierce competitor." Off the court: "He's one of these guys you love to lean on because he leans right back on you." On Pat Carroll: "He takes a lot of abuse from the bench because they believe he should make every shot." Off the court: Even with a house full of guests, "He'll just take us into the kitchen, and we'll talk . . . for hours." On Dwayne Jones: "Probably one of the most underrated players in the country." Off the court: "The most quiet guy I've ever seen in my life." On John Bryant: "A fiery soul waiting to come out." Off the court: "One of the funniest guys in the world. He can impersonate anybody." On Tyrone Barley: "I call Tyrone the Evil Empire because his defense is just . . . so mean." Off the court: "He's the St. Joe's . . . ladies' man."

I won't dwell on what Rob said about me. It included skillfully "walking that line between courtesy and being curt." None of these anecdotes is all that unusual in itself, just a typical group of college kids with very differing personalities. But put them together and what a team they made.

If you look at the official photograph of that team, you'll see sixteen players. Normally, we don't go beyond fifteen. You can't dress more than fifteen players in the Atlantic 10 Conference. Eventually, we redshirted freshman Robert Ferguson, which solved that potential problem. That there were four walk-ons is due to Jameer, and it's one of my favorite stories about him. A lot of people try out for our teams. Many played high-school ball with a good deal of success but just aren't up to Division I standards, and it's never easy to have to cut them.

That's the reason I started a junior varsity team at St. Joe's. These kids still want to be on a team that plays a competitive schedule against other schools On very rare occasions, a JV player has been moved up to the varsity. But no one is cut from that team, and they have a lot of cohesion and spirit. Still, anyone would prefer to be on the varsity, at least playing a lot of valuable minutes in practice. It looked like freshman guard Andrew Koefer, a pleasant, earnest, red-headed kid from Allentown who had tried out, just wasn't up to being on our varsity, even as a walk-on. We already had our limit of three, two of whom were seniors.

I asked Andrew to come to my office and closed the door, the sign to Clare that we were not to be disturbed unless it was something of imminent importance. I'm pretty sure Koefer knew what was coming. "Well, Andrew, you worked hard and tried your best," I started. I went on to suggest that he continue to work on his game, and come out again the following year. Then the phone rang. I thought this must be urgent, so I picked it up. It was Jameer. He asked whether that kid from Allentown was in the office, and whether I was about to cut him. He didn't even know Koefer's name. After I told him yes, Jameer, who'd never made such a request before, said, "I think you should keep him. He's a hard worker, and he'll help us in practice."

I asked Jameer if this was really important to him, and he replied that it was. So without telling Andrew who had called, I announced to the astonished freshman, "We've decided to keep you on the team." Here was our star player helping a kid he hardly knew. It says a lot about Jameer's character, reflected in the character of his teammates. He kind of set the tone. It also got us a lot of wonderful cookies from Koefer's grandmother. Maybe they're the crumbs Archdeacon was referring to.

As Rob's observations point out, a lot of very different personalities can come together to make an effective team. If, like my parents, you agree on what is most important, you don't have to all hang out together off the court. Your best friend might be someone with an entirely different background. That team had a lot more dash than flash. There was no trying to show up our opponents, no "woofing," no high-fiving, no trash-talking, just relentless play, sometimes with only one man in the middle, negating the stronger inside presence of other, bigger, but rarely tougher teams.

Among all the other memorable images I retain from that season, I love the one of Pat Carroll, caught by a photographer, actually jumping for joy—well, at least a bit off the floor—as his teammates rushed down the court after it was clear we were going to beat Texas Tech. We had some guys who were jumping higher, but that team never got *too* high.

It was an earlier phone call from Jameer, several years before, that really cemented in my mind what an exceptional person he is. We had been fortunate enough to find him early in the recruiting process, before the big boys closed in. I think he appreciated that, and remained loyal to us despite all the belated attention he was getting. I was winding up my fifth year as head coach.

As I've said, with outspoken, outstanding leaders like Mark Bass, our phenomenal two-year captain, and examples of character like Bernard Jones, my first year at the helm was very successful. So was our second season, 1996–97, when we won twenty-six games and lost only seven. I think of character players like Dmitri Domani, who came from Russia with virtually nothing (not even speaking English) and achieved so much, and Terrell Myers, who was immensely talented but who chose to come off the bench, sacrificing instant gratification for his team. He's playing in Europe now.

Like Mr. Chips, I reflect back on all my "boys." We had a guy on that team named Duval Simmonds, whose confidence had to be developed. His winning shots enabled us to claim the Atlantic 10 championship, and we went on to win two games in the NCAA tournament before falling to Kentucky. Great players like junior guard Rashid Bey and freshman standout Arthur "Yah" Davis were our scoring leaders.

Although we never lacked for talent, things didn't work out quite so well the next three seasons. I could empathize with Jim Boyle. I tried everything. We just weren't meshing as a team. Then I got that unexpected phone call from Jameer. He told me not to worry, that he was coming next year, and that we would start winning again. Just a few words—confident but not cocky. I could almost see that serious smile, if there is such a thing, on his face. Understand, he sensed I needed something to pick me up at just that time. Who is the teacher and who the student?

And, of course, in that next season, 2000–01, Jameer's freshman year, with Marvin O'Connor leading the way, we won twenty-six games and went to the second round of the NCAA tournament. We haven't had a losing season since. After all Jameer's honors (over twenty national awards) and being consensus player of the year in 2003–04, his number, 14, certainly deserved to be retired. He belongs up there with the Seneskys, Cliff Anderson, and Mike Bantom. We wanted to hoist his number, only the fourth to be retired in school history, up with the others in March 2004. But no, Jameer insisted, we had "more games to play." It was finally raised to the rafters on April 23, 2004.

Our team banquet that season was shared with our fans in the Fieldhouse itself. A sociology (not a basketball) major, Jameer put it best: "I wanted a great education. I wanted to be a role model. St. Joe's made all this come true. Coming back to school, this school, was the best decision I ever made in my life." I was not the only one who hugged him that night, and certainly not the only one who cried.

Rob Hartshorn had it right. I've learned something different from each of our players, over the years. Image aside, I'm churning inside before every game, and sleep less afterward. But competition was defined for me by Delonte West. He was fiercely competitive, and he hated to lose more than anyone I've ever been around. You wouldn't know it off the court. He's low-key, sensitive, fun-loving, and a really talented artist. Yes, he came from a tough background, but others who had it hard don't bring his passion to win. "How you played the game" may be most important to that final judge upstairs, but they do keep score for a reason. In business, you keep sales quotas for a reason. Having Jameer and Delonte together for three years was a blessing.

As I said at the outset, to treat everyone parentally is not to treat them all the same. Motivation wasn't much of a problem on that team. Guys like Dwayne Jones and John Bryant were low-maintenance self-starters. They didn't need to be pumped up. Every day they were in the gym, working out on their own. They might have liked more media attention on a team that featured Jameer, Delonte, and sharp-shooting Pat Carroll, but they never made an issue of it.

These players, over several seasons, just had a commitment to work. Basketball's a game each of them genuinely enjoyed. I've even had some of them say that our vigorous two-and-a-half-hour practices are actually "fun." I suppose preparation can be enjoyable at times if you enjoy the satisfaction of learning. Games are the tests you take. They are more serious by their nature. I know that working with that team was a joy. Work in itself is not the same as having a work ethic. Each of them had that attitude, from Jameer to the walk-ons—the desire to work on their game, to constantly improve. I do study body language. I do study eyes. I think they are the voice of the heart. Yes, Bobby Knight, I too like my players to look me in the eye. It often tells you just where that guy's mind is at.

Pat Carroll, who went on to have another spectacular season in 2004–05, is a true example of honoring your parents. He is exactly the way he was raised. I like to think I have some impact on every player, but he was formed before he got here. He influenced every one of his teammates, but never said a bad word about any of them. It may be that "soft-spoken" was one of the characteristic qualities of most members of that team. Pat only spoke at meetings when he had something to say, but as Rob put it, he could converse for hours at home or in a dorm room—the ultimate teammate, interested in what makes everyone else tick.

When Pat played, you just knew he'd be in the right spot. The shot might not always be perfect, but he was similarly exacting in everything he did. His game was smooth. The way he carried himself, just about everything he did was smooth—always calm and courteous, self-assured, true to himself, never flustered. You'd think that straight-arrow stuff might grate on some teammates who came from less secure backgrounds, but so far as I can see it never did.

That's the nature of a team that works. Of course, it's easy to be harmonious when you're winning. It's more difficult when you're challenged. In Chapter One, I said that after going to the funeral of Dwayne Lee's mother, our 2003–04 team became a family. Generally, I think it's a myth to label even the most successful teams as a family. In your family, living together, you know every member in depth, maybe sometimes more than you really want to. I think what you hope for in a team is a tight association of young people unified in a common purpose. Off the court they may go their separate ways. They don't have to all love each other, but they do have to respect each other and what they're about.

I think the beauty of almost all the teams I've had here is their willingness to give of themselves so that we can get better. That's what continues to excite me, encourage me, and make me believe—to build a program and not merely a team. But if any team was a family, it was those confident warriors of 2003–04, its members as diverse as my own family, but whose mutual bond transcended mere respect.

I could tell you stories about each of them. We had two foreign students on that team: Artur Surov, our sole senior last season, from Estonia by way of Finland and Georgia (our Georgia), and Arvydas Lidzius, from Lithuania by way of Maryland. Neither played as much as he would have liked, but there were no complaints. Would that the UN were so harmonious. Irrepressible Rob Hartshorn was our most excitable member. We knew when warm-ups ended because he'd dance round the circle at the center of the court. What a character. His enthusiasm for life extended to the team, giving it more energy. Brian Jesiolowski, another walk-on, was an excellent athlete and knew it, but he accepted his role, both giving and gaining respect. Steady Andrew Koefer and gregarious Rob Sullivan were our eyes from the bench. I'm glad I redshirted Rob Ferguson; we surely need him now.

Delonte hated to lose, but Tyrone Barley took it personally. Our best defensive player, he resented anyone scoring on him, even in practice. We all took our lead from Tyrone, intent on shutting the other team down. Chet Stachitas, an excellent student, has this inner drive that was never satisfied. A sharp-shooter like Pat Carroll, he would be especially effective in 2005–06. Dave Mallon, a former starter, fought injuries but did so many of the little things to help us win. As a talented inside player and good shooter, he had hoped for a much larger role. It must have hurt. A perimeter team, we could have used more help inside, but players like Mallon and Bryant never complained, nor did shot-blocking Dwayne Jones demand the ball.

Maybe they weren't that much like a family after all. They didn't bicker enough. When in talks after that season, referring to how our team had performed—sharing the ball, guarding, passing, respectfully playing the game in a way that I think people wanted to see it played, what coaching legend Larry Brown calls "the right way"—I described those players as the personification of teamwork. They weren't a collection of high-school Mc-Donald's All-Americans, but a team in every sense of the word.

I have all the respect in the world for Jim Calhoun, but after 2004 I'd say, "I know that Connecticut won the national championship, and they had a wonderful team. But I had the best team in the country that year." It was easily misunderstood, like some other things I've said, unless you think about what constitutes a team.

THE MOST PAINFUL incident I've had in coaching wasn't due to a bad call that cost us a game, or the result of some spontaneous overstatement of mine, but because of something another coach did—all the more painful because he's a man I've long admired, Hall of Fame coach John Chaney, then still at Temple. It was during the following season, 2004–05, when our depleted team, minus Jameer, Delonte, and Tyrone Barley but led by Pat Carroll, Chet Stachitas, Dwayne Jones, and Dwayne Lee, really overachieved, going to the NIT finals. As it turned out, we won that game with Temple, but that isn't what anyone remembers about it. Apparently, Chaney felt we were using an illegal screen, and the officials weren't doing anything about it. So he put in a burly, little-used player named Nehemiah Ingram to stir things up. I can relate to emotionally excessive language, but unfortunately Chaney later called his player a "goon." He came into the game very aggressively, but we'd coped with physical play before. And this guy was committing fouls, giving our team a better chance to win.

At the time of the incident, I wasn't immediately aware of exactly what had happened. I thought that on Chaney's part, putting this guy in said, in effect, "Look, I really want to win this game. I'll try anything," and on the player's part, "I want to impress my coach, and maybe get more minutes in the future." Then Ingram shoved our co-captain John Bryant, and Bryant fell awkwardly under the basket. We only learned later that his arm had been broken. At the time, there was so much anger stirring that the referees came over immediately to me, asking that I keep my team calm.

Retrospectively, I'm sorry I didn't respond more quickly after that game to Bryant's parents, expressing my concern. I was thinking more coherently after I left the arena that night. I'd been told that John Chaney had really gone off in his press conference, saying that he was an old-school "mean son of a bitch," and that he'd do it again if need be. I don't think illegal screens were the cause of his outburst or his actions. In my opinion, we weren't using them anyway, but I just don't think John was motivated by the tactics of our team. I believe, and I can relate to this too, he felt a heightened level of frustration because we'd beaten Temple a number of times in a row. They, too, are a proud program. Chaney's had enough of that.

Sometimes, however, when you're coaching against the same teams year after year, an impression may build that they play in a certain way, that some of their tendencies may even skirt the rules, and it's up to you to do something about it. It can make you a bit paranoid. Nothing out of the ordinary was exchanged between John and me when I saw him before, or even after, the game. Then, as I was leaving, when a reporter asked me about Chaney's "goon" remark, I was confused. I didn't directly answer his question because I didn't yet know all the facts, and I no more wanted to be disrespectful to a Temple player and his family than I would be to one of our own. So I kind of walked away from it, viewing what had happened as just an unfortunate incident in the heat of a tightly contested game.

The matter blew up the next day when I learned more. Our administration at Saint Joseph's was very supportive throughout, thoroughly behind our team, its coach, and particularly John Bryant and his family. Of course, as they say on the playgrounds, we hadn't started it. I was encouraged by our people to move away from the issue, not turn it into a major confrontation, and just concentrate on our team and the games to come. That would not be easy to do, once I learned that John Bryant's arm had been broken. A player from Temple had ended the career of a senior on our team, and I was supposed to keep quiet about it? What rubs me the wrong way in situations like this is when others comment without having the full facts. So, when I got nutty e-mails and letters from people implying that it was our strategy that had precipitated the incident, it was difficult to stay silent.

Twice I responded. Coach John Calipari of Memphis, a long-time friend of John Chaney's and mine (although years before, at a postgame press conference, Chaney had threatened to "kill" him), said publicly that the uproar about the incident was because "fair-haired Phil" was such a favorite of the media—that this whole mess was because of me. I called him on that, saying that it was ridiculous on its face. No Temple player had been injured.

Then there was an article in *USA Today*, written by an old friend of Chaney's, suggesting that five people were responsible for what happened that day—the three referees, John Chaney, and I. In response I wrote a letter to the author, an old-time basketball coach, saying bluntly that he had violated a couple of principles. Number one, if you never open your mouth, people won't learn what you don't know. Having opened your mouth, you proved that premise. He didn't know anything about what tactics I teach at our practices because he'd never seen one. How could he possibly assert in a national forum that illegal screens are the sort of strategy that is taught at Saint Joseph's? I have not spoken to him since. I don't normally hold grudges, but this goes beyond the pale.

As for Calipari, I did speak directly to him. He said he was just trying to be cute with the media. The old confrontation he'd had with John Chaney is still often shown on television. Although that outburst had done little to enhance Chaney's image, Calipari expressed how disappointed he'd been that no one at the time had seemed very supportive of him, its victim. It was Chaney, lovable but irascible, the old-school coach, vs. Calipari, who personified the slick, "blow-dried" coaches that seemingly now dominated the game. Apparently, his implication was that most everyone in this instance would support me because I'm a kind of media darling, good copy, and hardly "slick." So perhaps there should be a balance of blame, and so on. I still like and admire Calipari, but his reasoning in these circumstances was absurd.

As for Chaney, he tried to make amends, meeting personally with John Bryant's family. Undoubtedly, he sincerely regretted what had happened. I was, and to some extent still am, uneasy about it. John and I long ago went from being acquaintances to friends. Our teams competed against each other every year, vigorously but honorably, building mutual respect for the way we went about our work. He'd enjoyed a lot of success, but he cared about people even more than his program. We've long worked together on causes like Coaches vs. Cancer. No coach in this country has done more to help give young men, often from impoverished backgrounds, a chance to realize their dreams.

When Chaney would have one of these periodic outbursts—he believes passionately about everything from equal opportunity to national politics—the natural conclusion has been to view it as just John being John. He's done so much good for so long, why not overlook these occasional excesses? You have to take him as he is, and as for the media, his colorfully outspoken comments make mine look almost bland by comparison.

Yet, despite Chaney's record in creating opportunities and experiences for so many, his actions in that game resulted in taking the opportunity and experience of John Bryant's senior year away from him—and his family. Of course, we tried to make it up to JB. Senior Night that year was even more emotional than usual, but it wasn't the same as playing would have been for him. I still wonder. Had it been an instinctive action for John Chaney to send that player out on the floor to push people around, or did it stem from some deeper motivation?

Of course, I've seen Chaney since. He's normally such a likeable, congenial person, it's hard not to forgive him for a single incident during the heat of the game. But it's easier to forgive than forget. All I can conclude, after the interaction of so many years, is that what happened in that specific game doesn't represent to me the real John Chaney.

He retired last year. The Temple program is now in the hands of another fine coach, Fran Dunphy. He's also, at least "behind the mustache," a fierce competitor, but I hope there won't be any more broken bones when our teams meet in the future—just good, hard-nosed competition.

CHAPTER 8

Who's That Lunatic on the Tube?

Happy new year! January 2006 marked the start of the tenth anniversary season of *HawkTalk*. I suppose, particularly if you're not from these parts and you've managed to surf your way into the local channel we're on, that apparent "lunatic" you see must be me. Of course, you may also wonder about that jolly little elf sitting next to me, the enormous costumed hawk flapping his wings behind my desk, and why the giant TV is always on in what passes for our set. "Mabel, you've got to see this. What the hell do you think these guys are doing?" Could it be a rerun of the old *Gong Show*, the return of *Wayne's World*, or something new from Animal Planet?

Whatever we're doing, hopefully it's unpredictable enough for you to keep watching. Eventually you'll figure out that this is really a program about Saint Joseph's University basketball, but it definitely doesn't look or sound like any other "coach's show" you've ever seen—which is what we've had in mind from the beginning. As outlined in Chapter One, when asked to do a televised coach's show over a decade ago, I signed on—so long as it wouldn't be structured anything like the customary versions I'd seen. Of course, there are exceptions to everything. Villanova's basketball coach's show is great, mainly because of the hosting skills of Jay Wright, who does it straight. Most of them, however, rank just below real-estate listings in terms of any entertainment value and have all the spontaneity of synchronized swimming.

So here we were, after ten years, miraculously not only still around but flourishing. Oh, we do have some help. A professional production staff supplied by CCI Communications makes sure the cameras are on and that we finish on time. A few segments, like our "Martelli the Magnificent" and top ten lists, must be written by somebody, but beyond that we're still kind of making it up as we go along. Most of our shows are taped on campus before a reportedly live audience (sometimes it's hard to tell) and then shown later in the week. Our half-hour *HawkTalk* runs weekly between January and March, the height of our season.

Televised from Philadelphia on popular Comcast SportsNet, we're now also seen nationally via CollegeSportsTelevision (CSTV). I guess it didn't hurt when *The Sporting News* declared *HawkTalk* the nation's best coach's show. Consider the competition. We also do a weekly radio show live from a local restaurant—more focused on basketball. It runs a full hour, generally on Monday evenings, from seven to eight o'clock. We take calls, and I guess it's more predictable than the visual *HawkTalk*, but I hope no more pretentious.

Our tenth anniversary show began normally enough. My cheerily diminutive sidekick, Joe Lunardi, the world's foremost "bracketologist," introduced some of our impressively upscale sponsors, while a montage of former *HawkTalk* highlights lit up the TV screen. In some ways, we'd certainly come a long way. I think our first sponsor a decade ago was an unpainted furniture store. Our first "studio" was above a paint store. We were kind of into home improvement. Maybe Joe was so cheerful because he knew that no matter what he says, we can't afford to replace him. Smiling over at me, Joe reflected, "At first we thought we'd take advantage of your unique talents. Too bad that didn't work out." Which pretty much set the lighthearted tone between us.

Barbs aside, we were both appropriately formal in our tuxes. With his red bow tie, however, Joe looked like he just came from the Portly Tot Shop, and he still needs a booster chair. Since it was so special an occasion, we busted our budget to bring in balloons, a cake, and a parade of former guests, not all of them relatives. To get things off on a high note, I offered a million-dollar bounty to anyone who could prove they've watched every single episode of *HawkTalk*. Thankfully, we're still waiting.

Other than such special features, it was a typical show, although our audience did seem more animated than usual. Joe and I chatted a bit about sports in general and the fortunes of our own team in particular. Normally, we dwell more on future than past events; everyone pretty much knows whether we'd won or lost in the last week. But more than most, this particular show mixed nostalgia with the sophisticated schtick that has endeared us to a growing audience of admirers. Maybe it's more "endured" than "endeared," but *somebody* must be watching.

I didn't do my popular "Martelli the Magnificent" bit that night, our shameless takeoff on the old Johnny Carson *Tonight Show*'s "Carnac," but Joe kind of evoked it by asking what *Baywatch*, *Gunsmoke*, *Law and Order*, and *ER* all had in common. It turns out that they all had shorter runs on television than *HawkTalk*. Even *Seinfeld*, my favorite, signed off after nine seasons. At least *HawkTalk* is a show about *something*.

Over the years we've had remotes from locations as distant as the Wachovia Spectrum in South Philadelphia. Back in 2000, we sought out some really tough professional wrestlers (and they say we don't have professionals on our show) about to appear in *Monday Night Nitro*, guys like "Nasty Boy" Brian Hobbs and the "Disco Inferno," to give the Hawk some moves to take into hostile territory. All our mascot could do then came from "the Chicken" and John Travolta. Without a tag-team partner, the Hawk had to be prepared to take on all those really fierce mascots, like the Temple Owl and Penn's Quaker. Since these pros taught him a lethal move called "flap and slap," nobody messes with him any more. Unfortunately, there were no midget wrestlers to give Lunardi some moves of his own, but that show remains a fan favorite.

We're especially proud of our timely "interviews" with masked impersonators of such scary personalities as Saddam Hussein and Donald Trump. Saddam's mask looked more like Joe Stalin, but, as I say, we're a low-budget production. Anyway, my sidekick and I wound up pummeling the evasive Saddam with baseball beanbags. I wanted to hit Trump as well, pompadour and all, after all his unfortunate references to hairstyles. At least we got some information out of him about such vital subjects as his next nuptials—and the projected starting date for all those subsequent alimony payments. Blaming his problems on "the media," Trump wanted to fire Lunardi. That was the highlight for me. It's hard to capture all this classic television in print. You'll just have to watch it for yourselves.

Well, back to January 2006. It was on to our top ten list, an equally shameless steal, this one from David Letterman. As I recall, it went something like this:

THE TOP TEN HIGHLIGHTS FROM OUR FIRST DECADE

🔟 Governor Rendell names *HawkTalk* the best show televised from Philadelphia's City Line Avenue, narrowly edging out "Hurricane" Schwartz's Channel 10 weathercast.

❾ Joe Lunardi replaces Kathy Lee Gifford as my co-host.

❽ Lute Olson cancels his appearance on *HawkTalk* because of bad weather and the likely effect on his hair.

❼ Something about putting milk of magnesia in my coffee.

❻ The replacement of Crayola in our book review segment.

❺ Dr. Jack Ramsay, after his appearances on *Hawk-Talk*, denies any knowledge of Saint Joseph's University.

❹ Billy Packer claims *HawkTalk* just isn't up to the quality standards of the really major coach's shows.

❸ David Letterman's plagiarism suit is thrown out.

❷ The NCAA lifts its limit on how many *HawkTalks* a high-school recruit is permitted to watch before signing his letter of intent.

❶ I don't quite remember the specifics here, but it had something to do with the FCC and reruns.

If I seem a little vague about all this, the fact is that I've never actually seen *HawkTalk*. As noted, it's taped live on Mondays and aired later in the week. The hours vary, but it's suitable for all ages, unless there's some spontaneous slip-up, such as when I said "pimp" instead of "primp." Whenever it comes on, I'm probably watching tape of our next opponent instead. Yes, I have a VCR, but to me the fun is more in doing the show than in watching it, anyway. Fortunately, unlike in *American Idol*, Joe and I don't have to put up with three annoying judges to remind us that we don't have any talent. But I'm sure we have our share of dead air, boring chatter, segments that bomb out, and all the other pitfalls of what remains of live television. We don't do retakes. Maybe if I ever saw the show, I'd decide to stop it, even though it can be kind of a ball to do. But, fun or not, what has any of this to do with our team or our school?

Well, that's what sustains the show in my mind, the method to our seeming madness. You can't watch *HawkTalk* consistently without learning a lot more not only about our basketball program, but also about Philadelphia's own distinctive Saint Joseph's University itself. In whatever way, the more viewers we can capture, the wider that opportunity. There are a lot of other schools throughout America named for Saint Joseph, but only one that is an authentic university-level institution. By any measure, ours is a major academic entity—and getting better all the time. *HawkTalk*'s ultimate sponsor, after all those welcome ads for investment services, real estate developers, auto dealerships, healthcare, utilities, luxury resorts, and the like, is the university itself. I join in those filmed, informative commercials and really enjoy lending my voice to helping promote our shared vision: "Saint Joseph's . . . spirit, intellect, purpose . . . education with a conscience . . . this university is for winners—in the classroom, in the real world, in life." In short, that's what it's all about.

We wound up our tenth anniversary show with two interview segments—that is, of actual live people, not impersonators in masks. The first three guests had relevant ties to our basketball program and Hawk Hill; the other three represented the women in my life. Ray Cella, associate commissioner of the Atlantic 10 Conference, made his mid-season basketball predictions for both women's and men's teams, including the conference championships (I guess he was surprised later when we nearly beat Xavier). When he asked whether *HawkTalk* has created a stir at other schools, I suggested that, although we coaches are all copycats, there's no way anyone else can steal this idea. Anything this over-the-top has to come naturally.

Ellen Ryan is a wonderful person and a member of our Athletics Hall of Fame, who really put our women's athletics programs on the map, but she's not overly garrulous. Or perhaps she's just tactful. When I asked whether our show really "captures the essence" of our school, she just kind of smiled a hesitant smile. "Please," I pleaded, "this is a talk show. You have to help us out." Larry Dougherty, son of the legendary sports information director, historian, and SJU Hall of Famer Andy Dougherty, may have departed for Temple, but he retains his roots. He had more to say, although I enjoyed interrupting him by asking about Temple football, a program that, let's say, has been somewhat less successful than Temple basketball.

The three women in my life also tended toward brevity, although they should be used to live television by now. When I asked the indispensable Clare Ariano what's involved in preparing for *HawkTalk*, she simply said, "It's a lot of work." That's kind of the way it went. "Do you answer the phone like this?" I inquired. Judy, my wife of thirty years, was good enough to volunteer that our wedding, the birth of our three children, and her previous appearance on *HawkTalk* were the highlights of her life. Since we'd given her a metal walker on that occasion to mark her fiftieth birthday, I think she may have been expecting something more like a diamond bracelet this time. At least she hasn't yet thrown the walker at me, as threatened, and has yet to use it. Somehow we induce her to come back once a season for an update on things. When I asked what she looked forward to in the next decade of *HawkTalk*, she replied, "I hope you'll be funny." Our bright-eyed daughter, Elizabeth, nearing her nineteenth birthday, was the most animated, even though she said she hadn't been hearing very much about the program. She's probably spending too much time in the library.

As the show ended, all those balloons came down, just like at political conventions. I think afterwards Joe may have gathered them all up again to save for our twentieth anniversary show. I cut the cake, as all those former guests filed by in front of my desk, gathering together in a large group, glancing vainly around for any other refreshments. Looking at them through misty eyes, I couldn't help thinking about previous shows that had risen to equally high standards.

For example, here again were the three Phil Martellis. We'll steal from anybody, even one of the earliest black-and-white TV game shows. It was called *To Tell the Truth*. Three people would insist they were the same person, while a panel asked questions to determine which one was telling the truth and which ones were the imposters. With the last guest, a celebrity, the panel wore masks (here we go again). In our version, however, all three of the people claiming to be "Phil Martelli" were *actually* named Phil Martelli—me, my father, and a guy Lunardi happened to run into at a dinner. And here were all three of us together again. Now my father is no Clare Ariano. He can't stop talking.

On the original "Three Phils" program, Dad described, with his customary gift for details, just how he'd become friendly with this non-basketball Martelli, and then they both chimed in. It turns out both had wives named Mary or Mary Jane; they'd had children within days of each other; both loved to bowl, and on and on. Then ever-helpful Joe started in with his own questions, like, "How often are you asked if you're re-lated?" Finally I had to remind everybody, "Please. This is only a twenty-two minute show." I guess I was deducting commercials. Still, my father wasn't finished, wishing his granddaughter a happy birthday. That was nice enough. But we could've used a hook—or a gong.

For some reason, it's easier for me to remember parts of old top ten lists than other routines, but I do recall some that were related to the names of our players. Since we recruit just about everywhere, we've had some great names over the years. As "Martelli the Magnificent," that mighty sage of the East, I'd sit, just like Johnny Carson, wearing my own outlandish headgear, pondering intently and then coming up with answers to questions before I'd seen the questions. Then my sidekick, a cross between Ed McMahon and Austin Powers' "Mini Me," intoning "Oh, Great One," would ceremoniously hand me, one by one, envelopes containing the original questions. Here are a few memorable examples:

> **Answer:** Dorsal-like, to complete, and Artur's native tongue.
> **Question:** What is fin-ish, finish, and Finnish?

> **Answer:** Leonard, Chester, and Zippy.
> **Question:** What are three names Chet Stachitas won't respond to in practice?

> **Answer:** Spell Stacopoulis, Kapapoulis, and Kathopoulis.
> **Question:** What are the three final questions on the 2006 speech therapists' exam?

Of course, they're not all local references. Do you remember "J-Lo's favorite candy"? Naturally, it was "Low Pez." Since there is generally tepid applause for all this, until Joe announces, "I have in my hand the last envelope," I have to remind our audience, "Look, I don't write them, I just read them."

Later last season we had a top ten list of rejected names for *HawkTalk*. They included everything from *Hee Hawk* and

Hawk Soup to *Phil's Def Hawk Jam* and *Senor Phil's Universito* (our Spanish version).

Because our first show each season is in mid-January, both the fortunes of the Eagles and our own team are bound to be on at least our local listeners' minds. Back in January 2006, as opposed to this past season, the slumping Eagles didn't even make the playoffs. As for our own team, they were only 5 and 5 when they beat Temple by two on January 8, 2006. What seemed most consistent about them was their inconsistency. And how extremely quiet they were as a group—not just low-key, but really quiet. This time I didn't rise out of a coffin on the show to "wake them up," as I had during a prior season of *HawkTalk*, but Joe and I speculated about it. We'll try anything.

Ten years before, our team had come on pretty well—although the Eagles hadn't made the playoffs that season either, a rare occurrence. And here's a coincidence: After we noted that, energetic or not, our guys started playing more consistently, coming within one point of making the NCAA tournament and going to the second round of the NIT. What does that tell you about the inspirational impact of *HawkTalk*? I won't say coaches are superstitious, but I did once ask my own brother-in-law to stay home from games after we seemed to lose whenever he showed up.

Another popular feature has been the predictions of "Clare Voyant." I don't know how we entice people to return to our show, but however reluctant, Clare Ariano must feel it's her burden to bear as the bulwark of our program. Even though our budget doesn't provide for crystal balls, she comes back show after show, or calls in, to give us her remarkably accurate predictions for the Oscars, the Emmys, the Golden Globes, the NFL playoffs, you name it. The problem is, although her final answers are suitably succinct, she sits in silence thinking about them, as if there really is some inner voice trying to reach her. "Clare," I plead, "it's only a two-minute segment." I didn't know if she'd actually been to an NFL game, but she must go to the movies. She got nine out of ten of the Golden Globes right, for example, and I believe *Memoirs of a Geisha* was the only "foreign" movie she'd seen.

With the NFL it's even more remarkable. Clare's system is logic itself. It's the Steelers over Denver because, after all, Pittsburgh's in Pennsylvania. OK? She likes Baltimore's chances after I tell her their quarterback is still Johnny Unitas. I think she's into high-tops. Her winning percentage might be even higher if she didn't pick the Eagles every week. Pondering the divisional playoffs in 2005, she did admit that the Jets and Atlanta were just "feelings." She chose the Eagles, of course, despite not naming any of their players, and selected New England after hearing Unitas might be out.

It may be that because I've never watched the show, I remember particularly what we've done during the past two seasons. I will admit, however, that I've talked recently with people who *do* watch, to freshen up my memories. I recall, after telling Joe during one show that I'd asked our team to slow down during a game against 'Nova to boost our television ratings, we had a top ten list of "Things You Don't Want to Hear from Officials." They included: "Do these stripes make me look fat?" "I wish the pregame duck had been better, I feel a little funny"; "I think I just swallowed my whistle"; "It's God's will that St. Joe's loses"; "I'm not a ref, I just work at Foot Locker"; and, predictably, number one, "Oh, no, I forgot my glasses!"

We also had a top ten list of "Ways to Make the Postgame Press Conference More Exciting." They included using the *Jeopardy* format; putting the cameraman in the back on a unicycle; if you say "110 percent," you'll be shot on sight; giving each coach a choice of five mikes, one of which explodes; coaches get to tell reporters "Your momma is so fat" jokes; using our dance team as background for each question; a coach's challenge—

only to reporters; and number one: all participants must inhale helium before speaking. You just can't buy this kind of thing.

Probably my two favorite top ten lists were "The Ten Best Ways to Mispronounce Pete Kathopoulis' Name" (we'd better use him while we have him . . . and maybe Calathes, too), and my 2005 New Year's resolutions. Anyway, I've resurrected nine of them:

- ▸ Find somebody who can sing the national anthem the way it was written.

- ▸ Ask Clare to go back from blond to her natural hair color.

- ▸ Get our bus driver to give Andy Reid some advice for the Eagles, like he does for us.

- ▸ Make reservations for the Big 5 dinner now.

- ▸ Find room in our trophy case for some new trophies.

- ▸ Lose the ten pounds the camera puts on me.

- ▸ The only acceptable turnovers are apple turnovers.

- ▸ Win the *next* game.

And this was definitely number one:

- ▸ Hire some new writers.

Despite the hopefully comedic quality of all this, I think some of our most memorable *HawkTalk* segments were serious. It provides a good outlet for conversation, and continuity. In effect, the very lack of structure gives us the freedom to do what we want within any given program. Last season we showed a segment we'd taped with Jim Boyle back in 1997. He had just gone into the Big 5 Hall of Fame, and he recalled his childhood in West Philadelphia, growing up in the shadow of the Palestra. On his West Catholic varsity team there had been three outstanding future basketball coaches—Bo, Jim Lynam, and the record-setting Herb Magee of Philadelphia University.

At the time, Bo was an advance scout for what was then called the Washington Bullets, and he had accumulated something like 17,000 frequent flyer miles. He called me "one of the great point guards in the history of Widener University," but he was smiling when he said it. And he still used terms like "population density," more like a sociology professor than the customary coach. I recall we talked about his grandson, Brian, a promising player of whom he was very proud. I note today that John Griffin's oldest son is playing very well for Bucknell. Good genes.

Earlier that year, our guest was Dan Baker, longtime executive director of the Big 5 during its heyday, a true sports historian and gentleman of the game, and probably the finest public address announcer in the United States. Joe asked him, in anticipation of spring, to just give us a typical "now batting for the Phillies" announcement. He complied with "right-fielder Bobby Abr-eau." How time flies—he's now with the Yankees. Then, naturally enough, we dwelled on the Big 5, recalling some players who were never quite celebrated enough. He mentioned our own Mike Hauer.

Our talk then turned to recollections of Bo and what a great player he had been, not only a great person. "Do you remember back in the '60s that shot he made to beat Bowling Green?" Dan asked. Would that I had Dan's memory. And, of course, we turned to Bo's devotion to his family and how wonderfully supportive they were. "Tess," I agreed, "is on the express lane going to heaven." Whenever we reflect on Bo, it's sadness with a smile.

People don't normally come on *HawkTalk* to shill products, but it provides us with a welcome opportunity, amidst all our attempts at home-honed humor, to bring on guests who have something of value to say, or have accomplished something particularly admirable.

One such was ESPN writer Adrian Wojnarowski (*his* name should be on our top ten list), author of *The Miracle of St. Anthony*. It's simply a wonderful book—not a wonderful "sports book," but a wonderful book. Of course, I introduced him as an example of "shameless cross-promotion," since Joe Lunardi does his basketball bracketology for ESPN. Adrian's account of Bob Hurley's hard-nosed program, keeping alive not only the dreams of his players but the very school they represent in Jersey City, is both gripping and heart-warming. We've benefited from the talents and character of two of those players—Dwayne Lee and Ahmad Nivins, who's on our current team. Like Jameer Nelson before him, Ahmad stayed loyal to St. Joe's because we were first to seriously recruit him. I consider Hurley, a former parole officer who has turned down millions to stay in Jersey City so some of these kids could make it out to productive lives, to be one of the best basketball coaches in America.

Adrian told me the book may be turned into a motion picture, a sort of *Friday Night Lights* meets *A Season on the Brink*. I hope some of the profits will go back into that remarkable school. There should be more such feel-good stories. I appreciate having an outlet to promote them, and worthwhile causes in our own community.

Unpretentious Fran Dunphy fits that category. I don't know that anyone's done more to make our Philly 6 year-round Coaches vs. Cancer campaign the incredible success it's become. Of all the efforts throughout the nation, Philadelphia's events raise by far the most money for cancer research—reaching a million dollars a year. I remember playing golf once with Dunph when it occurred to us that there were lots of things we did normally that could simply be adapted to raising funds for this charitable cause—a Coaches vs. Cancer golf tournament, for example, or a dinner-dance. In this instance he was talking up a post-Selection Sunday breakfast for 700 people on the floor of the Palestra. What a great idea.

Dunphy was still at Penn at the time. As usual, his team was the first in the nation to earn a spot in the NCAA tournament. The Ivy League has no postseason tournament of its own. So Penn's players, and even their reluctant coach, were getting a lot of media attention. With unusual accuracy, Joe had them bracketed as a thirteenth seed. Of course, I needled Dunphy, "You're always sucking up to the media. You'd go to WaWa to get on their surveillance camera." As for his team, "Just think, you're as far ahead as the '64 Phillies." (For those of you who didn't read the earlier part of this book, they had a historic late-season collapse.) The fact is, Fran Dunphy, a Philly guy to the core, is an even better person than he is a coach.

I remember that during one show, when Joe and I were speculating about our Nielsen ratings, or whether we actually have any ratings, I told him that although I've never watched *Hawk-Talk*, I've also never actually missed a show. Since I think it's best live, a lot of it does live on in my mind. And besides, I didn't want to artificially increase our ratings by turning it on. Live or taped, as Joe put it, the operative word is "class."

When Joe was obliged to miss a show himself, doing his seasonal thing over on that other network, I actually had a full-size sidekick, Tom McCarthy, fill in. He's the play-by-play voice of our radio broadcasts and one of the best in the business. Joe Lunardi is his surprisingly good color man. On A-10 telecasts, Tom is supplemented by none other than John Griffin, who also does a thoroughly professional job. Tom looked great, having lost some 125 pounds, which gained more applause from our live audience than any top ten list we've ever had. I told Tom that since the end of *Seinfeld*, *Desperate Housewives* has vied with

Curb Your Enthusiasm as my favorite TV show. In recent seasons, if we start slowly, sometimes it's more like *Desperate Coaches* around here, with so many people looking over my shoulder to provide unsolicited advice. That's fine with me, so long as it's not relatives.

Tom was great, but he's used to playing it straight. Our guests were Jayson Stark, probably the leading expert on baseball in the United States, and then Seth Davis, an equally knowledgeable basketball analyst for *Sports Illustrated* and CBS. It was a pretty informative half-hour, speculating on the end of the college basketball season and the start of spring training down in Florida—always an exciting time of the year for sports fans.

Fortunately, Joe returned to the next show, bringing back our customary tone. Since that celebrated groundhog had seen its shadow, we looked forward to six more weeks of basketball. In our previous two games, despite both being wins, we'd turned the ball over thirty-one times. "What's our RPI?" I asked my regular sidekick. As usual, he didn't know, which is why I'd missed him so. "What's wrong with you?" he asked. "What's with all these basketball questions?" He was aware, however, that our team was, as the sportscasters say, winning ugly. The uglier the game, the better we seemed to play. That's OK, Joe confided, looking directly at me, "Even ugly men can have beautiful children."

Our guest for the first segment was radio sports personality "Jody Mac" McDonald. Maybe Joe had heard about the last show, which was so unusually informative. He and Jody Mac just started conversing so seriously about the whole spectrum of sports—football, baseball, and college basketball—that I began to feel like a spectator. At least it gave me a chance to do one of my classic Jack Benny "slow burn" imitations to the camera. I can run the gamut of expressions, as was once said of a well-endowed actress, from "A to B."

Our next segment was a bit more energetic and actually interactive, filmed at the impressive facilities of the Summit Sports Training Center. Under the guidance of Jesse Wright, St. Joe's strength and conditioning coach, each of us tried out equipment and exercises specifically designed for our needs. Avoiding the high-speed treadmill, I tried out what Jesse ominously called a "rock-back Russian twist"—I guess a kind of Dmitri Domani's revenge. The Hawk attempted a manual side-raiser while continuing to "flap and slap." For Joe, who asked in a matter of minutes, "When do we get a break?" Jesse had designed an apt "Bracketology Bridge." There was also a special squat for Steeler fans, but Clare wasn't around to try it out.

What brought us back, in our fast-paced fashion, to our makeshift studio was another visit by "Clare Voyant." Having found time to actually watch some games, she was ready to select her most valuable NFL players for the season. As I recall, they were Troy Polamalu and Hines Ward. Not bad. For the 2006 Super Bowl, she picked Pittsburgh over Seattle, "22 to 28 points" to 21. You see why we have more confidence in her than Lunardi with all his calculations.

Another way we're able to use *HawkTalk* is as an informative outlet for all kinds of people, in and out of athletics, to give us their views on things. I remember a great session with the colorful coach of our club ice hockey team, Finbar O'Connor. Even with a sport that gets modest campus visibility, Finbar actively recruits, and he's been immensely aided by the success of our basketball program. Like so many others who come from outside, he was also overwhelmed by how engaged (and occasionally enraged) Philadelphia fans are in sports on every level.

We hear regularly from the coaches of our professional teams, no matter how busy they are. One who stood out was the thoughtful Ken Hitchcock, former coach of the Flyers, who also came on our show. I remember he said that in over twenty years

Jameer Nelson setting it up. *Courtesy of Sideline Photos/ Saint Joseph's University*

Delonte West putting it up. *Courtesy of Sideline Photos/Saint Joseph's University*

Pat Carroll leads the leaping Hawks downcourt against Texas Tech. *Courtesy of Sideline Photos/Saint Joseph's University*

A season to savor: 2003–04. *Photo by Bob Coldwell/Courtesy of Saint Joseph's University*

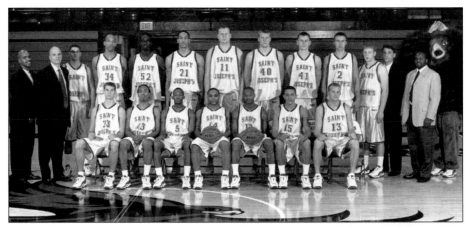

Courtesy of Sideline Photos/
Saint Joseph's University

The ultimate accolade: with
John Wooden in Los Angeles.
Photo by Marie Wozniak/Cour-
tesy of Saint Joseph's University

"The basket's that way!" Assistant coach Mark Bass. *Courtesy of Sideline Photos/Saint Joseph's University*

"Let's talk it up out there!" Assistant coach Dave Duda. *Courtesy of Sideline Photos/Saint Joseph's University*

"Look, at La Salle we did it this way." Assistant coach Doug Overton. *Courtesy of Sideline Photos/ Saint Joseph's University*

And the beat goes on...
Ahmad Nivins. *Courtesy of Sideline Photos/Saint Joseph's University*

Pat Calathes. *Courtesy of Sideline Photos/Saint Joseph's University*

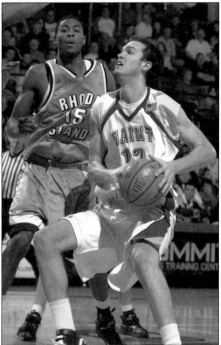

Rob Ferguson. *Courtesy of Sideline Photos/Saint Joseph's University*

The real "Dr. Phil." *Courtesy of Cabrini College*

HawkTalk's tenth anniversary. *Photo by Laird Bindrim/Courtesy of Saint Joseph's University*

United we stand: "Philly 6" Coaches vs. Cancer. *Courtesy of American Cancer Society*

Heart of Hawk Hill: Don DiJulia, Clare Ariano, Ellen Ryan, and Chris DiJulia. *Courtesy of Sideline Photos/ Saint Joseph's University*

Our future home: the renovated Alumni Memorial Fieldhouse. *Rendering by Burt, Hill/Courtesy of Saint Joseph's University*

But one thing you can always count on: "The Hawk Will Never Die!" *Courtesy of Sideline Photos/Saint Joseph's University*

of coaching he'd never seen any place like Philadelphia. It's "unique in every aspect . . . it's black-and-white. Fans don't gloss over when you're not working. It's the most competitive city I've ever seen, the only city in America that is so tied in to sports . . . . The lid would blow off if the Eagles won the Super Bowl."

Or, I might add, if we'd won that NCAA championship in 2004. Well, at least we still have our own hockey puck in Joe Lunardi, and our dreams never die. I started off the 2005 season of *HawkTalk* insisting, "I don't care what Comcast has coming on next. Cancel it! This show will have the highest ratings of the year." We certainly had some unique settings that season. We did one entire show from inside a brand-new Mercedes Benz. Most of the time I was trying to keep Joe outside it, fearing his fiddling around would turn it into a "used" car.

One of our longtime sponsors, the Pennmark Auto Group, had suffered an extensive fire at their Fort Washington showroom and used our show to demonstrate that they were still very much in business, and committed to the same high standards. Stressing that "you have to be surrounded by winners to be a winner," I talked with people sitting in the seat next to me from their ownership, sales, and service departments. One guy, who'd been working there some sixteen years, suggested that I'd probably had more hair when he started. Who needs Lunardi? When I finally, reluctantly, emerged from that luxurious car to remind viewers of our upcoming schedule of games, I felt we'd put in a full day, but I kind of missed our live audience of students and staff.

I don't want to single out specific sponsors. They're all great—and created equal in our hearts and coffers. But I do think Joe had a crush on that attractive young woman who was featured on the Gladwyne Concierge commercial. Every time she yelled into the phone, "Wow! You're fantastic," he just kind of lost his focus. You devoted viewers know that he always comes up with a unique way to introduce each show. "What could be better than a perfect season?" he exclaimed in January 2005. "A *new* season of *HawkTalk*." Then Joe and I actually talked seriously for a while. The whole preceding year had been magnificent not just for us but for the entire Atlantic 10. Now we were about to start over, "using last season to feel good about ourselves."

Of course, the first half of this new season had already concluded, but our league schedule, as usual, would be largely in the second half. Of necessity, this was more of a learning year, with different kinds of practices, less stop-and-go, and more individual instruction. The games right after exams, always the most difficult, would be especially challenging. Lunardi suggested, "You're really earning your salary this year." Well, I said, "We can't miss opportunities. Even on *HawkTalk* we have no backups, only starters. So you're our jockey for this race, Joe." Back to form. "You've had an entire year to think of something original to say," he replied, "and that's the best you can come up with?"

I think the shows that have stayed most in my mind, without the need for others to remind me, and really what *HawkTalk* is most about, are the concluding programs each March. Their focus is on the seniors who are leaving our program—not only the players but the managers, interns, and often the Hawk. They are also the most rewarding programs for us to do.

If you think about it, the months just before graduation from college are among the most traumatic in a young person's life. Sixteen years of certainty come to a too-sudden end. For those of us who went to preschool, even more. From our earliest recollections, next September school would surely start again. It might be in a new setting or on a different level, but there was always that certainty, whether looked forward to or only anticipated. Now our classes are at an end. There will be no papers or exams next semester, and, sadly, no spring break next March.

If our first team was family, leaving home to go to college surely represents a major transition, a new level of independence. But it's not nearly so sudden or final as the end of school, breaking the ties that have defined our lives. It's like concluding a career, but you don't retire in your twenties. Those who go on to graduate school are a minority. For most of us, exciting or ominous, it's the biggest change we've yet known. It's so abrupt, this transition from certainty to uncertainty. As I read in a yearbook entry, "We'll have these moments forever, but never again." "What are you doing next year?" one senior asks another. "Well, I'm not really sure, but let's keep in touch." On your own at last. What's out there? Is there a job?

Maybe that helps explain why it can be so hard to speculate about it in a setting like *HawkTalk*. What's tougher to talk about than the future? And it also helps explain why so many students, here as elsewhere, just decide to hang around for an extra year or so before easing out of this secure environment they've known, for the unknown. The future may seem bright, full of promise, even limitless, but it's also scary as hell. At least for many of our players, they've the option of continuing for a few broadening years to play the game they've known all their lives, wherever in the world it might turn out to be. And what's more broadening than seeing new places?

Co-captain John Bryant, on *HawkTalk* in March 2005, didn't fully project on camera the spontaneous, spirited guy we'd all come to appreciate. As I said when I introduced him, no one had added more class or dignity to our program, or made it more enjoyable to be around. Although he admitted to having watched a few *HawkTalks* in the past, he'd not been a regular viewer. There's a lot to do as a student-athlete, or simply a student, at Saint Joseph's. Having received his bachelor's degree in 2004, John was already working toward a master's in business administration. No one doubts his future success. He couldn't come up with one specific memory that stood out in his college career. "Hopefully," he said, "every day has been memorable." His senior year was one of special challenge, overcoming severe asthma and, of course, that incident in the Temple game that put him out of action. At times, he said, he was bound to wonder, "Why is it always me?" But I don't think he has many regrets.

Our other co-captain, slick-shooting Pat Carroll, had rushed from class to make what turned out to be a one-minute appearance on our final *HawkTalk* of 2005. "What you've done for our program is so great," I told him, "and now you get on *HawkTalk* to top it off." Like Bryant, he smiled ruefully, but that was about it. Thankfully, I'd get to see both of them a lot more before graduation. Pat still hopes to play in the NBA but is currently with a team in France. Wherever he goes, I don't think anyone needs to worry about his future, any more than Bryant's. I wouldn't mind promoting these two guys as the poster boys of our program, and would love to see them back on our show, with more time, more memories, and more laughs.

Talk about diversity. We had some real characters as managers that year, primed to move on to bigger things in their lives. There's no way to overemphasize the importance of good, well-organized managers on a basketball team. No program can run smoothly without them. Many people knew Chris Napoli, our head manager in 2004–05, as "Hammer." I had to ask him, "What the hell is your *real* name?" In his "career" prior to St. Joe's, Hammer was a rapper in his parents' garage. His departure for our campus may not have been all that tearful. His current group has a CD out called "Dirty Jersey." Apparently, he's now known as "Nap Daddy." His post-graduation plans? "I'm just going to hang around for a while."

I don't recall ever seeing his associate, light and lively Kelly Ann Grace, with shoes on. "Flying Toes" wore flip-flops throughout all four years. Naturally, she prefers Jimmy Buffett's music to Chris Napoli's, and had some vague plans to go down to Key West, work for Pat Croce, and watch the sunsets from Mallory Square. We'll have to catch up on just what happened. Like Mr. Chips, I like to stay in touch. Mike Tecce, our departing Hawk (this season it's Jim Miller, the thirtieth student to serve as college sports' most energetic mascot), is off to law school at Villanova University. Well, it figures—since, as I suggested, "You failed the SATs." Maybe it was all that flapping. But he might yet make something of himself.

The amazingly energetic Caitlin Ryan finally fulfilled her lifelong ambition to appear on *HawkTalk* in 2006. She served as a student manager for two years, graduating in 2004, then for two years was our director of basketball operations, and has received her MBA. I've no doubt she'll wind up as a major player in sports management, probably something like succeeding Phil Knight at Nike. Her GPA at Saint Joseph's is reputed to have been in excess of Joe Lunardi's height. It's just nice to know that some people actually *want* to get on our show. Rob Sullivan, who succeeded Caitlin as director of men's basketball operations, a multifaceted responsibility, is almost her equal in upbeat energy, if not in intellect.

Well, from Tom Durso, the guy who spent one whole program just heckling me, to a show featuring both author John Feinstein and Governor Ed Rendell, from the three Martellis to the one Vince Papale, the SJU alumnus whose inspirational story formed the basis for the movie *Invincible*, our eleven years had been quite a run—with no end in sight.

What I've concluded is that *HawkTalk* isn't really a "coach's show" at all. At the outset, I didn't want it to be a *typical* coach's show. Now I realize, as it's evolved, if that's the word, that it isn't about me. I'm simply the co-host, trying to keep things moving along. *HawkTalk* can be as wacky as I'm sometimes reputed to be, as cheerful as Joe, or as thoughtful and informative as many of our guests, from inside and outside our school and its basketball program. Doesn't that in itself say a lot about our administration, so reflective of their own comfort level and trust that they'll let us put on this show just about any way we like, or however it turns out? In the final analysis (no, not "the end of the day"), this represents our small window into what makes Saint Joseph's University what it is. I hope it's the welcoming window we all want it to be.

CHAPTER 9

Ten to Take with You

I DON'T BELIEVE YOU CAN LEARN HOW TO LIVE, HOW TO LEAD, OR even how to love—from a book. And, to answer a question I'm often asked, you can't learn how to coach from a book, either. With no disrespect to their prominent authors, I have no single favorite book by an influential basketball coach that has most shaped my own way of working. I believe I've learned something from all of them, none more than our own Dr. Jack Ramsay, both in the context of coaching and the greater game of life itself. Who knows more about building a "pyramid of success" than John Wooden, or about the "key words" that underlie success more than Mike Krzyzewski?

In a sense, *each* of us is a book, encompassing our own lessons to impart—and our own approach to life's challenges. Unfortunately, most people never get around to writing them down. Just as each of us has the capacity to coach, we each represent a unique story of accumulated experiences. Every person you meet is a book you can benefit from. You need only be receptive enough to keep your antenna up, and your shutter open. I'm reminded that the show *Cabaret* was derived from a book called *I Am a Camera*. I try to read a lot, but learning also involves the record our mind retains of what we see and hear from everyone we meet.

As a coach, every clinic I attend and every videotape I review is a window into another coach's world. In effect, he's reading to me out of his own book. I try to visualize what his life is like. It's not unlike being immersed in those detective and mystery stories I enjoy for recreational reading.

Of course, I'm also frequently asked if I've developed a "Martelli method," my own special style of coaching strategy. I'm not that smart. Like most other coaches, I'll borrow from anyone who has experienced success. I try to take something from many sources and adapt it to the talent we have. Our 2003–04 team, for example, generally featured four guards playing at the same time, and pressed relentlessly during at least the first half of most of our games. It worked because they were really good at it—and, more importantly, were committed to keep working to get even better.

What do you define as coaching? If you think coaching is putting an X and an O on pieces of paper and moving them around, I've no unique way of doing that. But if you believe, as I do, that coaching is relationship-driven, organizing and motivating, I *can* do that. And if you give me enough time, I think I could learn to do it in the corporate world, as well. Coaching to me is not about the strategies. Of course, you need a working knowledge of them, but it's more important to have a vision. You have to look at that videotape and say, "This is what I see that may help me." You have to be able to look at each player and grasp what is happening to him, what he's likely to be able to do. Of course, you can be wrong, and on occasion I have been very wrong. But to me, the distinct systems in basketball are few and far between.

There was Dean Smith's old four corners, the Temple match-up-zone, the methodical Princeton man-to-man offense, Bobby Knight's man-to-man defense, Paul Westhead's racehorse basketball. They're all systems. I feel comfortable enough to say that I don't have such a specific system. But I do have an ego large enough to believe I can always find a way to adapt what I do have into a winning strategy. To me, if you have a set system, your team in year five may look the same as your team in year one. And your team in game twenty this season will look like your team did in game two. I know enough to be pretty certain that's not the way teams, or people, develop.

That's not to say we have no basic formula for winning. It's rooted in the thoroughly planned practices that underlie our program—everything timed, everything competitive. Yet you can't overload players. It's a delicate balance. Be prepared, but not over-prepared. Don't look too far ahead. We have a day a week where we do review, so that our players never feel that they've been overwhelmed. I want to teach different combinations because you're never sure what's going to happen. And then two days prior to a game, whether it's considered the biggest game of the year or it's the very first game of the year, that's when we start preparing for a specific opponent. In 2003–04, we coaches had already done a lot of our mental preparation before our players heard the names of Xavier or Gonzaga or Villanova or Oklahoma State. So whatever you do, whether you're a physicist or a coach, you need an overall formula. When I go in on Mondays, I have my formula for that day. I can tell you what we try to accomplish with our off days, our formula for weight training, our overall philosophy for winning—which, little by little, we introduce to our players as their confidence grows.

I guess you might label our style of play as the "Martelli mix." Our teams tend to have a lot of motion mixed in with some set plays. Whether we stress man-to-man defense, zone, fast-break, full-court, three-point shooting, crashing the boards, or the back-door cut at any given time is based on the situation and the talents and tendencies of the players we have to work with—mixing, matching, and molding their individual skills into the most effective team we can put out on the court. Is it any different in business? You have people who can sell, and people who are better at planning. There is even such a thing as creative filing. Without a strong support staff, your stars aren't going to score often enough to keep making the sales that will grow your business. Everyone in your company will follow someone who knows where he's going—a head coach who can communicate a plan yet be flexible, demonstrate interest in every player, maximize their skills, and motivate them to do their best as a team.

Whatever I've been able to accomplish within what amounts to our own modest company originates from observing and adapting what has worked for others. In some ways I'm still that insecure high-school coach who whistled his first team to practice—only now I've been shaped by thirty years of experience. You may be the CEO of an infinitely larger enterprise, but, as I said at the outset, hopefully something from these experiences of mine may resonate in helping you to meet the challenges you face every day. There's no other way I can justify the presumption of giving advice in this conversation with you.

A lot of it may seem obvious, and much of it has already been touched on. But I'm going to try to compress these principles that matter to me into ten points—my message from the hardwood to the hard world we all face. I like to think of it as a lesson plan for life.

1. All wins are not winning experiences; all losses are not losing experiences.

As Jameer said after that most agonizing of losses three seasons ago, he didn't feel like a loser. The members of both teams had left it all out there on the floor, where Jameer remained in stunned disbelief. They had poured out everything they had to give that day. On the other hand, we've had many victories where the standards of how we practice weren't met. The result may have been momentarily positive, but the process was less than satisfying. We've all experienced fortuitous success based on doing less than our best. If that leads to letting down, it will result in future failure, when there may be more at stake. Our number one goal is not winning; it is to get better each day. In our case, it is to be better as a team in March than we were in November.

Most important, every member of *your* team has to feel as if he or she played a recognized part in achieving your shared goals. I'll never forget when I was a high-school coach, where everything I've learned was nurtured, how hard it was to look into the eyes of a kid who hadn't played, even if we'd won that particular game. Did he feel himself to be a real member of our team, or simply an adjunct? Of course, those practices, where he sweated as much as any starter, formed the framework of our success. But how to convince *him* of that? His dream was not to be a practice player. I hope I've gotten better at this over the years, to make everyone feel part of the team. A teammate's value is based less on minutes in the limelight than on commitment before the lights go on. I want the experience of every walk-on to be as great as that of a starter.

And, of course, taking the long view is vital. If you came in second for that contract you were counting on, and which everyone on your team worked so hard to get, swallow your disappointment and stay positive. I believe that demeanor should all but guarantee your status as a solid competitor for the next contract, and the next. If your goal is to do better every day, winning will come. I think it was Winston

Churchill who said, "Success is never final. Failure is never fatal. The only thing that endures is character."

2. To get respect, you must first give it.

This idea should be as self-evident as "life, liberty, and the pursuit of happiness." Our society has gotten excessively hooked on possessions and positions, on things rather than values. Your title does not automatically confer respect, nor does your job description, your advanced degree, or your high credit rating (although it's nice to have). No matter how exalted your status, you can only earn respect by extending it to others. Early in this book I mentioned a definition of character as showing the same face to everyone. Not treating them all the same way, but extending to each the same level of respect. The author of that definition went on to say: "Never patronize people just because they can help you, or be abusive to them because they cannot." Only if you've earned the regard of your secretaries and janitors, of everyone from the boiler room to the boardroom, can you view yourself as a successful executive.

I was fortunate in growing up around parents who extended respect to everyone they met. One thing I observed at an early age was how much they listened. Other than showing up on time, that may be the ultimate sign of respect—actually caring enough about what other people have to say to listen to them, and then to talk *with* rather than *at* them. Such sensitivity can't be faked, but like any form of self-improvement, it can certainly be developed. I spend a lot of time around people with far more formal education than I've had. Almost invariably, the most renowned are the least pretentious. They rarely hide behind titles or accolades.

Materialism may be more rampant in the business than the academic world, but you can bridge the widening compensation gap we all read so much about by showing genuine interest in what everyone in your company does. Get down from the tower to spend some valuable time with them, listening and exchanging ideas. You may find that by earning the esteem of others, you'll wind up discovering what is best in yourself.

I've mentioned how poor my memory is. It hasn't been easy learning to retain the first names of so many people I run into, and details about their lives. It has, however, been among the most rewarding experiences of my life. Listening doesn't come all that naturally to me, either. If I've been able to develop a more discerning ear, surely you can, too.

3. Every day be willing to teach; each day be open to learning.

How do you draw a line between teaching and learning? I've noted that great people, whatever their field may be, tend to be great listeners. They are not great "hearers." There is a difference. We have a lot of noise at our practices, for example, and much more at our games, but I try not to hear it. My focus is on what needs to be done and what needs to be said. The outstanding leaders in any field are not necessarily eloquent, but they have to be able to clearly articulate what they mean, and get others to respond to it, overcoming all the extraneous noise around them. To gain attention, you have to think and speak on your feet—and choose the right words.

In his new book, political researcher and strategist Frank Luntz has some interesting observations about this idea. It's called *Words That Work: It's Not What You Say, It's What People Hear*. Particularly in these times, voters seem more motivated by perceptions of authenticity than by ideology or even issues. Luntz cites Ronald Reagan as a president who communicated effectively through storytelling, and Bill Clinton, who mastered a convincingly conversational style. Yet in the past, Dwight Eisenhower and Harry Truman, neither great orators, were clearly understood by the electorate. The very words we choose to use have meaning and power. For example, "estate" or "inheritance" taxes imply that only wealthy people are involved. "Death taxes" include everyone. Luntz is very critical of the speaking skills of most major business leaders. There isn't enough emphasis on how to communicate clearly and convincingly. For example, especially when you address larger audiences, aim your remarks not to the people closest to you but to those at the rear of the hall. If they respond, your message is getting across.

My direct audience each day at practice is only seventeen people—fourteen players and three assistant coaches. The time I have to communicate with them is always too short. I try to have specific messages for individuals who need to hear them. Hopefully, they have also been listening to each other. I learned from my high-school teams how positive peer pressure can be. A player who has earned enough respect to call another player out represents a learning experience for the person strong enough to issue the challenge, and the person strong enough to accept it as positive reinforcement.

Even as we teach, we are learning from each other. It took me a while to realize that less is more, to keep things simple. The fewer rules the better in any organization. The most important rules in mine have always been to be on time and to be prepared. I don't want to operate as a policeman or a judge, but more as a counselor. No, you can't treat every player (or every employee) in precisely the same way. Particularly with young players, some need a hug, some a nudge, some a pat on the back, some a rhetorical kick in the rear.

What you *can* be is fair. If you've got too many absolutes, you'll paint yourself into a corner. It's better to establish standards you set together. I think when most of us start out in teaching, coaching, or in the business world, we want to have an answer for everything. Eventually, we find that we don't. It's OK if the answer is "I don't know" or "I'll find out." That's acceptable in any form of management, part of the honesty that earns you the respect of people who look to you for leadership.

How often we hear that those who will not heed the lessons of history are fated to repeat them. We teach so little of our own country's unique history and heritage today; it can be surprising to many even well-educated people how relevant its lessons still are to whatever they are engaged in. Recently, a prominent motivational specialist took a group of bemused executives on a tour of the Gettysburg battlefield. Technically, the North won the battle, but General Meade's failure to follow up his victory allowed the Southern forces under Lee to escape, and that prolonged the Civil War for another bloody two years.

On their thorough tour of the battlefield, the businessmen learned not only which of the commanders was indecisive and which too aggressive, but how a hundred lesser decisions, many of them spontaneous, by those well down the chain of command, really determined the outcome. That clarity made it a day few of those executives will ever forget—and that each will profit from. I wish our recruits knew more about the history of our program—not that it would help to determine their decision, but it might enrich their experience.

Certainly, coaches or executives in any field need the ego to feel that they can do it better than anyone else. But the years teach the difference between confidence and cockiness. From Mark Bernsteil I learned not to make decisions too hastily. From Johnny Custer I learned about perseverance. From so many of my high-school players I learned about representing something greater than yourself. From those first Kenrick players I learned about patience. From Bernard Jones and John Bryant I learned about forbearance. And on and on.

I've learned from those who rarely left the bench, and from those who went on to NBA careers. There was an effort to move our last regular-season game in 2004, because it would be the culmination of a perfect regular season of 27-0, to the immense dimensions of the Wachovia Center or Spectrum in South Philadelphia, with all of the attendant national hoopla it would garner. Normally, our Big 5 games are played at Penn's Palestra, our second home. But this contest, on March 2, 2004, would be against St. Bonaventure, our final regular-season Atlantic 10 match-up. Jameer Nelson and Tyrone Barley, who would have benefited from the exposure of such an expanded venue, wouldn't hear of it. They wanted to play their final home game at Alumni Memorial Fieldhouse in front of those 3,200 frenzied fans who had been with them every step of the way. And so we did.

I hope every player benefits from his time on Hawk Hill. I know I have. I've learned a lot about character.

4. The success of a group assures the success of an individual; it is never the other way around.

Life is a group activity. Self-centered people believe the spotlight shines on them specifically. You don't want them in your company. We don't want them on our team.

Before Jameer and Delonte there was Marvin O'Connor. A marvelously gifted athlete, he still owns the Saint Joseph's record for most points scored in a season, 706 in 2000–01. More significantly, he led a fine team, including Bill Phillips, Na'im Crenshaw, and, in his final two seasons, Jameer Nelson as well. Although as a transfer O'Connor had to sit out his first year, he scored a total of 1,678 points over only three seasons at St. Joe's. He was a definite NBA prospect with a decision to make after his junior season, not unlike those later faced by Jameer and Delonte. Even the most high-profile programs boast relatively few such prospects.

A single game, the conclusion of his most successful season, thrust Marvin into the consciousness of basketball fans throughout the nation. After winning twenty-five games in 2000–01, his junior season, O'Connor led the Hawks to a first-round NCAA victory over Georgia Tech, 66 to 62. Highly ranked Stanford was next. With St. Joe's seeded in the West Regional, both games were played in San Diego. Over 11,000 spectators witnessed a pulse-pounding struggle only slightly less tense than the one three years hence. Stanford led by nine at the half, but the Hawks fought back, led by O'Connor's five treys. By the time he fouled out, he had scored 37 points, 15 of 20 field goals. The crowd, predominantly favoring Stanford, gave him a standing ovation. Stanford won by seven. Not all losses are losing experiences.

But one look at Marvin's face demolished any hint of personal satisfaction. It was as drained of emotion as Jameer's would be three years later. Sitting dejectedly on the bench as the Cardinal players celebrated their triumph, Marvin O'Connor was the leader of a team, and his team had lost.

Some people believe that then and there Marvin decided that he had to return for his senior season, but it is not so. In the hyped excess of big-time sports, with the line increasingly blurred between college and pro, both the NCAA and the NBA came in for considerable criticism. So do we college coaches. Why shouldn't we want our most productive players to return for their senior seasons—or, in some well-publicized instances, even their sophomore seasons? Of course we do, but the team is more important than any individual. And in determining what is best for that individual, we're not relying only on our own instincts.

The NBA provides us with an evaluation of whether a player will be drafted, and roughly where. You get a letter from them each year asking, "Do you have any underclassmen who you feel have pro potential?" We submitted Marvin's name to their Underclassmen Advisory Committee to make their evaluation. They responded with the opinion that Marvin was most likely to be taken somewhere in the second round, something less than a prime prospect. He might be better served by coming back to school. After that determination, he and his family had a difficult decision to make. He could take a chance and pay his way to a no-obligation pre-draft camp and possibly impress coaches sufficiently to improve his positioning. If he wants to test the waters, but not hire an agent, a player retains his right to return to school the following year.

As it happened, however, that was the last year underclassmen had to pay their own way to these camps—no small investment. After weighing his options, Marvin decided to return for his senior season. Of course, his teammates were happy with his decision, and so was I. I've never pressured a student-athlete to return, but every decision entails risk. In retrospect, the result of Marvin's decision may seem a sad story, but life doesn't end on the hardwood. He had developed debilitating injuries—turf toe, and ankle and foot injuries that considerably slowed him down. His senior season, stressful for anyone, was one of decline, although the numbers were still impressive. Our team went 19 and 12, with O'Connor leading them to the second round of the NIT. His average of 17.5 points, down from 22.1, still led our scorers; his rebounding and foul-shooting actually went up.

I believe that had Marvin's shooting statistics remained constant, some NBA team would have overlooked his injuries and drafted him. He had played just as hard as a senior and would likely have been at least a productive role player in the pros. But he never played professionally. Sometimes the harder we try, the heavier the load becomes. All I recall is that wonderful talent and drive. I just wish he'd received the chance he deserved. Today Marvin is employed at Philadelphia's Youth Study Center, doing worthwhile work as part of a different team.

It is the success of a group that assures the success of an individual, but individual decisions can be very important to keeping that group together. Jameer Nelson's decision was anything but easy. The NBA paid his way to Chicago, and we were told that he "might" be a first-round pick; he'd played very well. We gathered as much input as we could, but the decision was entirely his to make. Certainly, Jameer's returning for his senior season was significant. Even the way he told his teammates, at first solemn and then surprising them with a grin, betrayed not only his playful nature but how close he felt to each of them. When their magical ride together ended, it was teamwork Jameer reflected on, and his teammates—Delonte West, Pat Carroll, Dwayne Jones, Tyrone Barley, and all the others.

Even after West, too, had departed for the NBA, what happened "the year after" (as imprinted on all those T-shirts) and the year after that, with diminished talent available, demonstrates the vital value of teamwork. The remarkable run of our 2004–05 team, 24 and 12, led by sharpshooters Carroll and Chet Stachitas, culminated in another tough loss, this one by three points, to South Carolina in the final game of the NIT at Madison Square Garden.

Perhaps the even more remarkable success of our balanced 2005–06 team, devoid of standout stars, clinches the point. Denied the opportunity to go back to the NCAA tournament by an even more agonizing single-point loss to Xavier, they returned to the NIT, losing to Hofstra by two in the second round. At least this time it was in front of our own appreciative fans at the Fieldhouse. What was it Kipling said? Face triumph or disaster, treating those impostors just the same. It's not all that easy.

It was Delonte's matchless will that motivated his decision to forgo his senior season. Both Delonte and Jameer have very strong mothers. Their means may have been limited, but not the affection that instills in a young person the desire not to disappoint others. I wasn't raised in so tough an environment, but I hope I can relate to their decisions. It may be too much to say that Delonte had to win, and Jameer had to play, but I think that in the final analysis, Jameer returned for his senior season because he simply loved college and college basketball. He knew he had a future in professional basketball, but there were other things he wanted to do first, like leaving a legacy here. He didn't need instant gratification. The money could wait.

Delonte is a very bright guy, very gifted artistically. But he was never crazy about school. His focus was on four o'clock. That meant competition, and that's what he lived for. These two young men were great teammates, but quite different personalities. Jameer was very open from the outset. You had to earn Delonte's trust, but once given it would always be there. I would never bet against either of them. This may be viewed as my program, but it will always be their school, and that of their other teammates. If I helped open some doors, that's what I'm here for.

Delonte was not so highly ranked as Jameer, but he knew he was better than the projections. As it turned out, he was taken in the first round of the 2004 NBA draft, only two places behind Jameer's twentieth selection. Of course, that only motivated Jameer's equally restrained resolve to prove people wrong. He starts for the Orlando Magic today and is emerging as a star in the league, while Delonte is playing for the Seattle SuperSonics. No surprise to me, or to them.

Jameer's falling to twentieth, after being hailed as the player of the year by everyone except *Sports Illustrated* (they named Emeka Okafor) was viewed generally as a disappointment, for him and for us. That misinterprets things. He was drafted. A lifelong dream was fulfilled that night. His name was called, and then Delonte's, by the commissioner of the NBA. There are thousands of kids who dream of that, and it happened to them. So whether they were fifth or tenth or twentieth or twenty-second doesn't matter. Two dreams were fulfilled. How often in our lives can we say that?

I don't think there's a college coach anywhere who doesn't want to see his players graduate. Most of ours do, but few statistics can be as misleading or as easily manipulated as graduation rates. It's a number that understandably enhances your accountability to your university. But it's only a number. Bear in mind, however, the minute number of students who are on our basketball teams. If only one transfers, or only one leaves early, how does that affect our graduation rate as against that of the overall student body? "All of our seniors graduated," we hear proud coaches proclaim. Well, high-profile athlete or not, how many seniors at any college or university fail to graduate? The more meaningful statistic, of course, is how many first-year students went on to graduate?

The NBA's new ruling that no one can enter the league prior to his nineteenth birthday pretty much eliminates kids coming directly from high school to the pros, but it guarantees that a lot of "blue chippers" will play only one or two years of college ball. Just take a look at how this affects teams as they advance to and through the NCAA tournament.

Much as I want every student-athlete we recruit to stay a full four years—I like to think even more for his benefit than mine—I believe the quality of his experience with us is more important than the quantity. With so much emphasis on high-profile college sports, it is fashionable to blast the NCAA for its apparent emphasis on trivial rules and its avoidance of major issues. I'm not frequently accused of patronizing the powerful, but I do believe that overall they're doing a good job of dealing with difficult problems, and, in fact, have made great strides in recent years. How would I change some of their restrictions? Well, rather than limit the time I can spend with the young men who play on our teams, I'd like to see it expanded and made more flexible, especially in working with individuals.

To my knowledge, no recruit has ever come to Saint Joseph's because of its graduation rates (high), any more than because of its basketball heritage (wonderful) or the state of its facilities (improving). I think parents and coaches want most of all to know that we'll work one-on-one with their kids, including areas beyond honing their skills on the court. The memorable mentors of my childhood, the Tom Gallaghers, really widened my horizons, using sports to enhance growth and development. They supplemented the example of my parents. We may be dealing with a more self-centered generation today, but that only heightens the challenge.

The fact is that most of the young men we wind up getting at St. Joe's are very similar to those we've had in the past. What has changed since 2003–04 is that our school gets more immediate recognition, and so do I. Jim Boyle and John Griffin probably had to work a lot harder in recruiting. I can get into most doors. Many of the kids we meet have been understandably spoiled by so much attention, used to getting what they want rather than what they need. Not everyone will fit into our framework.

"Parental" is a word I've used in this book almost as much as "passion." Sometimes it can be very valuable to a young person's development just to say "no." But if they are as coachable as most of our recruits are, they will appreciate our candor as well as the one-on-one attention. We want them to really develop their skills instead of coming into a program and stagnating. Being supportive may not mean catering to a recruit's every whim, but I'll bet our approach would work just as well with a McDonald's All-American or two.

I think that every opportunity you have to guide someone is a teaching moment. If, say, a student is gifted in fine arts, and we have an outstanding painter on our faculty, wouldn't anyone interested in education favor them spending as much time together as possible? And the growth every teacher aims for is not limited to a student's specialty. If physics majors, English majors, or business majors are free to work on joint projects with their professors, before or after class, in or out of the formal academic calendar, why should that opportunity be denied to those who happen to play sports? Anything we can do to enhance the student-athlete experience is worth the effort.

I'm a teacher. Teamwork may be what I stress, but learning is mostly about developing life skills. There's no cookie-cutter identity that says "basketball player" or "basketball coach." There is a lot more I'd like to learn as well as teach—yes, maybe even how to use a computer. The college presidents who run the NCAA are smart enough to work out a way to increase access in both directions. Who ever concluded that spending too much time with a productive teacher will reduce your chances to graduate, or to succeed in life?

I have a lot of commitments, but I can always find time to invest in what is most important to what I do. If I can spend an extra hour or so each week to work individually with a player, or if he has the option to come by occasionally during the summer, I believe it will benefit us both. It may or may not improve his jump shot, but I'm also confident enough to hope it may help him grow as a person, essential to everything we define as education. Wasn't that the main reason his parents entrusted him to us in the first place? What such access will *not* do is overload his single-minded emphasis on basketball.

To me, numbers need to be accompanied by words, and words by meaning. If you're with us for only two years, do you go around with the equivalent of a scarlet letter saying "fifty percent"? When we play a game, the numbers too often stand alone. We either win or lose. In business you either made your sales quota or you didn't. But did you improve? Consider the rates and percentages. Are you getting better? Was our team better in the fourth quarter than the first? At the end of the season, let's hope that we are playing our best basketball. Let's hope that by the end of the academic year, whether it's your first or fourth, you're a better student than you were at the start. At the end of this quarter, let's hope you're a better salesman than you were when it began. And hopefully, after your second—or thirtieth—year of marriage, you should be a better husband or wife than you were in your first year. So to me, it's always about this day and this day only. As philosophers have said since Roman times, "Seize the day!" You might want to add: "Live in the moment."

I believe that in higher education we're responsible to make a better student into a better person. It can't be scientifically measured. You have to experience the person. Are such persons getting better at time management? Are they more respectful of others? Are they more comfortable in public settings? Are they more confident? A lot of this development occurs outside the limitations of books, blackboards, and PowerPoint presentations, beyond band practice and shoot-arounds. You can see it in dorms and cafeterias, through community service, a host of activities, and one-on-one interaction. I can't speak for other universities, but I like to believe we're good at it here.

Your own team is composed of individuals. How they interact will determine the success of the group, and how you go beyond coaching and dictating to motivate each individual to make that group stronger will determine your own success.

5. Don't take yourself too seriously.

I could write a whole book on this subject. In a manner of speaking, I suppose I already have. If I've still any tendencies toward excessive self-importance, it never takes long to run into somebody who will bring me down to earth. For example, last summer, in boarding a plane, a lady I'd never seen before thanked me profusely for deciding to stay in Philadelphia. She had been told something like, "That coach is on this plane." It took me a while to realize that she thought I was Fran Dunphy. The fact is, I think I look more like Jay Wright, but so much for semi-celebrity.

Yes, it does take some ego to coach any sport successfully, but I think mine was at its peak three decades ago when I started out at Bishop Kenrick and was so full of myself. The size of my ego has declined a bit every year since, as experience has taken over. I'm proud that my assistant coaches there—Geno Auriemma, Bob Mullen, and Tom Grady—are still close friends. Another, Tommy Kehoe, is my brother-in-law. Confidence is not the same as conceit. It helps in keeping a sense of proportion to learn and stress what you have the potential to be good at—and, however well-intentioned, to stay away from what you will only mess up.

As I've said, overall my memory is terrible, yet I can recall specific dates with the accuracy of "Martelli the Magnificent." My first official date with the lovely Judy Marra was that football game at Franklin Field. The second was going to the movies. That particular film was called *The Other Side of the Mountain*, a poignant real-life story of a young woman, a champion skier, who was paralyzed in a terrible accident. I was so affected that I had to leave the film in the middle. I all but passed out in the lobby, was revived, and got back to my seat about half an hour later.

Instead of fearing she'd been dumped by her oddball suitor, Judy discovered he had the emotional consistency of a jar of Smucker's. Well, I understand that General Grant got queasy at the sight of blood, and he still won a few battles. At least I don't pass out during games, but after, say, the twentieth turnover I still feel myself getting squeamish.

It's easy to say this now, but I recommend big weddings, even if you have to borrow the money. Don't wait until you can afford it to appreciate it. Judy and I had a wonderful wedding we'll always remember. We both come from large families and didn't want to exclude anyone. Of course, it helps to have the certainty you'll only be doing this once. I don't really forget her birthday, as we've pretended sometimes on *HawkTalk*, but I'm not likely to forget the day we got married. We met in June, were engaged in December, but didn't actually wed until November 20, 1976. Since we were both coaching, we couldn't set the date at the height of our seasons. Love and basketball.

It's amazing that our marriage has survived so many mishaps. Intending to be a modern, share-the-chores husband, I wanted to help out with everything. Unfortunately, my first effort at cooking involved putting a frozen chicken into the oven and setting our kitchen on fire. After a call to 911 saved the rest of our house, I never cooked again beyond the still-scary use of a microwave. You have to know what you're good at. I've never quite trusted technology, although there isn't much consistency to my convictions. I believe the computer is a fad, and have never learned to use one. However, to me the cell phone is the greatest achievement of our times. It may seem excessive that almost every student I see has one permanently affixed to his or her ear, but I couldn't function without mine, especially now that they're so small.

Then there was the dishwasher incident. By then I should have known better. It was on Valentine's Day—Judy was sick in bed and our kids were still at school. I managed to get home early enough to try to help out by doing the dishes. Since naturally I put hand soap in the dishwasher, our entire kitchen—not the one I'd burned in Norristown; we'd moved to a larger house in Drexel Hill—became full of bubbles. All I could do was wade through and call the kids. I was too embarrassed to try 911 again. Then there was that incident with a hot water heater in the basement, and all the times I've needed first aid. Kitchens are lethal. Let's just say that I finally understand that I'm handier outside the home.

I seem to remember someone, I think her sister, telling me that Judy said as a teenager that she wanted someday to marry a man who loved sports and didn't smoke. She didn't say anything about hair. Anyway, she's not only achieved such laudable objectives, but now she shares them with three very sympathetic children. They've all played on teams, and I don't believe they've ever smoked.

Elizabeth, our youngest, was a three-sport athlete at Merion Mercy Academy, although an ankle injury precluded her pursuing hoops at college. I think it may have been more her social life, but we're not into investigative reporting here. She's majoring in elementary education, but I suspect, like her brothers, may actually do some coaching before being swept off by Mister Right. An oversized ego is no longer an option for me. My whole family understands enough about what I do to bring me back to a sense of proportion very quickly.

The most important asset you can have for success in any field is a supportive family. Often I read about prominent coaches in all sports who simply burn out. I can only speculate why. With all their rewards, was it ever enough fun? Was it shared? However success is measured, you can be—in fact, you almost have to be—totally committed to what you're doing. However, to pursue your passion, you needn't be consumed by it. As our children were growing up, all five of us were rarely together at the dinner table at the same time (even though I was no longer cooking). Out-of-town trips often precluded my attending their important events. Inevitably, I missed occasions significant to all of us. But we got together as often as we possibly could.

Judy and I never pushed our children into liking basketball. They might have hated it, since it kept me away so often. Instead, they just came to enjoy being around the team, visiting my office with their mother, becoming part of what their father did. Elizabeth, as a little kid, was almost adopted by the players. They called her "Pinky." She got to travel all over the country with us, and to Italy on our summer tour.

Judy and I tried to emulate our parents in being neither excessively permissive nor controlling, but I will admit to a sense of satisfaction when today our kids view us as devoted and involved parents. Elizabeth even called me "affectionate." It's not a question of putting your family ahead of your job; with a healthy family situation they coexist. Life needn't be a trade-off. I'll never regret driving three hours to see Jimmy play at Dickinson or having Phil Jr. by my side on the bench at Saint Joseph's, despite all the taunts by opposing fans. It comes with the territory. And how great it is that some twenty-eight relatives still come to every home game, now once again including my brother-in-law, Ed David. I told him at Christmas dinner in 2003 that he was welcome to return. No one was likely to jinx that particular team.

My intention to remain a regular guy, however, hasn't changed my game-day rituals. Judy may still roll her eyes, but she understands as only a onetime coach could. We're told in the book of Ecclesiastes that to everything there is a season. On game days I'm not quite the same person as on other days. I see each game as a test for the players. Whenever you have a test in life, in school, or in your business, the preparation is more important for the teacher, the coach, the person in charge. The test is for the players, the students, the salesmen. The best teachers don't run up and down the aisles in their classrooms, shouting to their students during a test. So it is a habit that I try to take from practice to remain calm during games, at least externally to my players. Calmness breeds confidence.

By the morning of that contest, however, I'm a nervous wreck. By game-time I'm churning inside. It's less in terms of whether or not we're going to win than whether I've prepared our players to do their very best that day. Of course, if they do, we *should* win. After detailing our strategy in the locker room, I'm the last guy out on the court. Again, it's not ego. I just want a moment of solitary reflection.

Once the game starts, I try to stay relatively calm, almost professorial, my hands clasped across my chest or behind my back, pacing a bit, with a serious expression. It's not always successful. What I view as a bad call can lead to confrontation with a referee, a botched play to a few pointed words to that particular player. But overall, I think it's important that every player pick up that demeanor of calm confidence from their coach. I don't think it's deceptive to try to keep the churning internal. At least I'm not yet hooked on antacids or sedatives.

Throughout game day I prefer to be entirely alone. If it's a home game, I stay at home until departing for our field-house or the Palestra. Everyone knows not to disturb me. I may seem to be resting on the couch, but of course I'm not sleeping—I'm thinking of potential game situations. Again, it's less ego than focus. If it's a road game, I do what has to be done at the shoot-around, but even at the pregame meal I may only be there for three or four minutes. I don't talk very much to anybody on game day. My assistant coaches understand this as well as my family. No matter what, we're going to have overlooked something. You have to learn to accept that.

I follow so set a routine that it's bound to seem superstitious. I lay my clothes out, and always dress at the same time of day. Fortunately I can afford more than one suit now, or I'd always wear the same thing. At home or away, I make certain notes at certain times of the day. When I go to the locker room, there's a set of prayers that I always say to myself. The same rosary is always in my pocket. I don't pray for victory; I pray for us to do our best. It all has a calming influence on me. I know by then what I want our players to do, and pretty much how and when I want them to do it. So do they. Even if everything gets thrown out of kilter, it shouldn't cause paranoia. As Churchill said, who can predict how the fates will play, mocking all our hopes and dreams? I've done my best, but whatever happens, worry will always be a part of this profession.

Our bemused managers will tell you they've learned to live with it. I always park my car in the same spot at home

games, and the same comfortingly familiar Bruce Spring-
steen CD is always playing when I arrive. Recently, with my
car in the shop, I made sure to get another copy of it to play
in the rental car on my way to the game. And there are other,
similar rituals. All right, I suppose it *is* superstitious, but
there's nothing wrong with regularity. Postgame, win or lose,
is kind of like an astronaut's debriefing. First a few words to
the players, then the press conference, finally back home to
Media. Judy will call me to bed, knowing I'm not likely to get
there until four or five a.m. I'm replaying everything in my
head, just as I'll soon look at the actual tapes.

Does this make the whole process of coaching a college
basketball team far more important than it is? I don't think
so. Within the overall scheme of things, whatever we under-
take in life, we want to do as well as we possibly can. As for
those whose efforts we may supervise, we want them to do
as well as they possibly can. We and our players and our fans
certainly hope for it, and my job may ultimately depend on
it, but the goal isn't really victory. The goal is to achieve excellence, or as close as we can get to it—like that game
against the Bonnies when their fans got so angry at me. If
you're not passionate about what you choose to do in life,
find something else.

I don't think that after most of our games the players
would tell you that they thought I was nervous. Perhaps
upset at times, even angry at their perceived lapses, but not
really nervous. There's a regular routine behind this, as well.
Everyone may have to step up and be a "play-maker" in a key
game against Xavier, for example. But I try never to overemphasize the importance of one game or de-emphasize another. They are all important. The Las Vegas line means
nothing to me. I think that in playing basketball, as in life, the
task at hand is always the most important one. Earlier in this

book I cited one instance when I departed from this premise, thinking too far ahead, to our team's detriment.

Every game matters. I don't like to say, "Take one game at a time," but it's one bromide that holds up. Whether you're selling an account that's worth $50,000 or $500,000, every proposal you make is worthy of your best efforts. It equally represents the stature of your firm. Reputedly, when asked why he never let up in a game, Joe DiMaggio said, "There may be a kid out there who never saw me play before."

I don't think it's more important to teach preschoolers or sixth-graders than twelfth-graders or college seniors. Who's to say what juncture is most pivotal in a young person's development? And to repeat that premise: Since the best teachers don't run up and down the aisles shouting at students, why do we coaches think that is an appropriate response to circumstances we can't control?

Take what you do seriously, not yourself. Life's not only too short, it's too unpredictable. Keep it in balance. *The Human Comedy* isn't simply the name of a play.

6. Who you are is more important than what you do.

It means more to me when people say, "We want our kids to go to your basketball camp this summer" or "We'd like you to speak at our next luncheon" than "We think you're a great coach." I'm not a professional camp director or public speaker. But if someone has heard that our summer camp is the best, or that I gave a speech somewhere that people remember, it not only reflects favorably on the university I represent, but I hope it helps define the kind of person I try to be.

Coaching basketball is my profession, and I put everything I have into it, but it doesn't define who I am. Whenever I'm asked, in effect, "Why are you always promoting yourself?" I reply that my motivation is not to promote myself but my school, and the values it stands for. You'll have to take my word for it. I'm not complaining about all those personal appearances and the time they take. I enjoy them, but they are not to enhance my self-esteem.

The greatest compliment anyone can receive is that he or she is a good person. At the end of your life that is what it really comes down to—what people will cherish, remember, and take with them. Every day, consciously or not, you're working on the kind of person you are. In school the accolades go to the best students, the best athletes, the leaders, the high achievers. Those kids get the respect of their peers and the deserved rewards that entitle them to stand out, to make their parents proud.

Selflessness, generosity, and service to others can be harder to quantify. That is what I try to stress when I talk with students, on whatever level, which I do as often as I can. As I've said, "no" has never been a large part of my vocabulary. If I talk for, say, forty minutes with a group of basketball players, no one is likely to become a better player in so short a time. Hopefully, however, they may pick up some nugget to encourage them to become better people.

It is easier to give a eulogy than a commencement address. For one thing, you are likely to know the deceased well enough to find something positive to say about him, or recall some anecdote about an experience you've shared. Despite the somber nature of the occasion, a bit of levity is as welcome as brevity. "Yes, he was like that," people will recall, if you've done a good job.

Even if your own child is involved, you're not likely to know very many of those young people you face at a graduation exercise. Whether you do or not, one thing is uppermost in their minds: how to get out of there as quickly as possible. The deceased at a funeral has already departed. At university and college commencements, politicians and other notables receiving honorary degrees have been known to exploit the exposure for policy pronouncements that have nothing to do with the matter at hand. Even if the graduation speaker sticks to laboriously wishing everyone well, it can be a pretty tedious affair.

Among the few people I've heard who are good at making relevant commencement addresses are Bill Cosby, who personifies brevity and levity, and Ed Rendell, who conveys a genuine enthusiasm. More frequently the audience can't wait to hear "Godspeed," a word only used at graduations, which means their ordeal is at an end. A similar tradition is "without further ado," a phrase only used in lame introductions, even by prominent people.

What I try to do before any audience, especially a student audience, whatever the specific occasion, is to turn the focus on them, and the kind of people they should strive to be. They're not enamored with what I do for a living, anyway. I'm just one more middle-aged visitor, today's time-waster. "What makes a real person?" I ask my youngest audiences. Let's spell it out. It should be someone with *p*ride and *e*nthusiasm, who accepts *r*esponsibility, is willing to *s*acrifice for others, takes advantage of *o*pportunities, and says *n*o to negatives. "Whether you know it or not, every day you're working on who you are. Try to be a better person each day." At least it's a little like *Sesame Street*. In the 1920s there was a popular self-help guru who told his adherents to chant, "Every day in every way, I'm getting better and better." It can't hurt, so long as actions follow words.

Surrounded with people who hold doctorates and other "terminal" degrees (there *must* be a less ominous way to put that), I like to say I'm proud of my *two* doctorates. That both were honorary doesn't diminish their value to me, especially since they came from two institutions I think so highly of. Of course, when each was awarded, by Widener University and Cabrini College, it involved my giving a commencement address. Because a lot of people have been good enough to comment on my talk at Cabrini, I'd like to say a few words about *those* few words that I directed to their graduating class of 2006.

You may not have the opportunity to make such a specific speech, but communication is the key to motivating in any situation, whether to a sales force, a family, or a student body. As always, brevity and at least some levity are helpful. These young people, like all graduates, are focused on the future, their own immediate future—having a blast and then getting a job. Anxious to "commence" with the next stage of their lives, potentially they're what any performer would consider a "tough crowd."

Nevertheless, I think it doesn't hurt to reflect with them not only on the future but on their immediate past, what they've shared together. Within their ranks are so many people, not necessarily the most recognized, whose activities provide hope for their future, and ours as a society.

First, however, I asked all the graduates to complete "one last assignment"—to thank their parents for everything they've done with a standing ovation. "A parent holds a child in their arms for a short time," I noted, "but in their hearts forever." I went on to pose the question on everyone's mind: "Now what?" We each faced a dilemma—mine to hold their attention; theirs, what to do with the rest of their lives. "Let's make a deal," I suggested. "If you've any ideas, give me a call or a text message, and I'll try to say something worthwhile."

The point, I think, as with any audience, is to try to engage their attention by being direct at the outset. Throwing in a surprise doesn't hurt, either—even if it's as hokey as the sales manager who offered ten dollars to anyone who would come up to join him on the platform. Moral: "You have to get up off your butt to make a buck."

Then I went on to cite the experiences of those representative students. Cabrini College means a lot to me because it's where my youngest sister, Lisa (no, not the one who's funnier than I am), really blossomed to become the accomplished person she is today. I told her story, and proceeded to briefly tell the stories of those others, each of whom was graduating on that day. Even while wondering and worrying about "now what" in terms of their own lives, consider how much so many of them had already done. There was the young woman who started a life-skills program for troubled teenagers, the guy who gave up athletic eligibility to pursue his MBA, the senior who hosted a fair-trade Christmas sale, the campus leader who drove the baseball team's bus because somebody had to.

The award-winners at commencement may have expected recognition. It's not likely that each of these people did. I don't think other students or their parents resented these few being singled out, reflecting credit on all the graduates. All it entailed was some prior questioning of the school's "underpaid" (I promised I'd get that in) faculty and administrators. In speaking to any audience, I think getting some positive reaction can be a combination of forethought and spontaneity.

I went on to the points I always stress and have stressed in this book: coaching throughout life, maximizing skills, organizing, building relationships, how the success of the group assures the success of the individual, working to become better than you believed possible, dreaming. "I hope that in your coaching you experience the thrill of victory, the lessons of losing, and the incredible joy that comes with the pursuit of excellence." I cited a last example: "Matt Grzeskowiak seems to have adopted this philosophy in his work with the Wolfington Center Programs . . . Matt, I would have mentioned you earlier if I could pronounce your last name"—and finally I congratulated all the graduates and wished them not "Godspeed" but God's blessings.

Of course, they will always remember this bright day in their lives. And even if they little noted nor will long remember what I said to them, I also treasure the time we spent together. Not as basketball coach Phil Martelli, not as someone who tried to be funny or eloquent, or was honored that day—just as a friend of the family who hopefully, like everyone else, keeps trying, stumbling, and then trying again to become a better person. Who you are is more important than what you do.

7. **We have no more right to someone's time than we do to their money.**

The memory of specific dates is part of our national consciousness. Sadly, they tend to be days of disaster or shared mourning. No one alive today is likely to forget September 11, 2001. People of my generation still recall where we were when we heard the news from Dallas on November 22, 1963. Our parents will never forget December 7, 1941.

The personal dates we retain within our own family circle are more joyous—birthdays, weddings, special celebrations—but they also include the inevitable deaths of those we loved. In the cycle of life, time is our most precious commodity, even if we don't dwell on the grim reality that it is constantly running out. Things are only "set in time" in the clocks of our memory. There is only so much we can squeeze into a day. How we use what we have helps make us who we are and helps determine how we affect others. In any group activity, being on time may be the ultimate sign of respect, but the person keeping the clock has to justify it.

In retrospect, I suppose my own "day of infamy" would have to be October 15, 1979. Imagine someone with my memory still recalling it so vividly. In my mind it still matters. It was that first day of practice at Bishop Kenrick High School, the experience I keep coming back to. As their newly hired twenty-three-year-old head coach, I knew everything. I was now the resident Naismith Memorial basketball genius. We practiced for three hours and ten minutes, longer than I do with my players today. I returned home still full of myself, until I began to think about the practice on the next day, and the next.

At around five a.m. I sat up in bed, fully awake. I realized that I had told my players in that one session just about everything I knew about the game of basketball. The rest of that season I was flying by the seat of my pants, with no overall plan or purpose, simply running one drill and then another. I may not have been literally stealing money from these kids, but I was certainly stealing their time. I was letting them down, and they knew it. Not being prepared to coach them more effectively remains the greatest single regret of my life. I've described how I went to Cathy Rush with my dilemma, and how she set me straight. But it was too late for that particular team.

Fast forward to October 25, 2006. My numbered practice plan for that afternoon (and every practice every season) in the Fieldhouse had a pervasive theme, "Know-Trust-Execute," and everything was timed to the minute. Unless there was a compelling reason, everyone on the team gathered here at four, ready to go. Between 4:15 and 4:17, we exchanged thoughts, coaches outlining what we wanted to stress that day. The next eight minutes were devoted to stretching. Then four minutes for the "Celtic warm-up drill." We coaches did some pushups on our own, and a lot of running. I can use it. Did I say coaches borrow from each other? Between 4:29 and the end of practice at 6:45, defensive and offensive variations running from two minutes to twelve included references to drills labeled for Michigan State, Connecticut, Penn State, North Carolina, the Nets and Spurs of the NBA, not to mention simply "Pitino" and something I won't try to describe called "Blob/Slob." Sometimes it looks like organized chaos, but the key word is "organized."

In retrospect, we probably should have spent more time practicing foul-shooting and trying to avoid turnovers, if that's possible. I don't know how similar our practices are to how other teams do it, but I suspect we may have a slightly more competitive environment, more noise, and more animation. For one thing, we try to approximate something of the atmosphere of a real game. Anyone is welcome to come in and watch every practice we hold.

On the day I recall, female students were running up and down the stands for exercise, the JV team came in to look (presumably at our practice, not the female students), and my dad, as always, was watching from the top of the stands. So was Garrett Williamson's father, getting his basketball "fix" for the day. When kids' teams show up, we can have hundreds of spectators.

Sometimes I feel like the ringmaster of at least a two-ring circus, standing at mid-court and focusing one way and then the other at our squad, now split into two teams, each guided by an assistant coach. Between position work and "stations," team "A" and team "B" play each other, one approximating our next opponents. This is supplemented by individual instruction and a lot of encouragement. By the time practice is over, Mark, David, Doug, and I are probably at least as tired as the players, and only one of us is over fifty. No plan can be perfect, and at Saint Joseph's academics come first.

On the day I remember, Marcus Mitchell came in at five, his class not over until 4:45; Artur Surov had to leave at 5:45 for his next class. Arvydas Lidzius was too sick to make it. But all the other players were there for the duration, almost as energetic at 6:45 as at 4:00. Of course, it's a young team.

Ever since that first season coaching high school, I've never held a practice that wasn't scripted minute to minute and scheduled weeks in advance. I'm not completely inflexible. No realistic coach can be. We may have variations of emphasis in mid-season, based on how things have gone and what needs to be worked on most, but my overall practice schedule is completed before the season even starts. There are books about the joy of living, the joy of loving, even the joy of cooking. You'll have to take my word for it—there is genuine joy to being well organized. In any aspect of the real world, I'm convinced that being organized is the foundation that fosters the development of everything you want to become.

Yes, I'm often checking game tapes at five a.m., and compiling lists of reminders to myself via my trusty Dictaphone, but I'm not married to every detail, and in practice itself, showing some flexibility or sharing decisions doesn't mean the abdication of authority. It's healthy. What might individual players want to get done today, especially upperclassmen, the experienced leadership of the team? And unless there are special circumstances, the door to my office is as open as our practices. I'm married to only one person, not to every iota of my lists.

There are people who believe that college players in the extremely rigorous major "revenue-producing" sports should be paid some spending money, say $100 or so a week, beyond their full scholarships—in that their commitment to their program is so total it precludes things like work-study or the part-time jobs available to other students. This isn't the venue to really debate it. I'd only suggest that much as I want our teams to be successful, if the commitment of individual players is so absolute that it overwhelms everything else they should be getting out of being here, there's something out of whack.

Again, I can only speak for my own school. Everyone who plays basketball at Saint Joseph's should have the same opportunity for as fulfilling and rewarding a total experience as a student who chooses to play tennis or soccer or plays in the band or writes for the school newspaper or is active in student government. We may not all be equal in our ultimate success, but we should all be equal in opportunity.

Whether, in effect, we take your parents' money in tuition, or you're on full scholarship, or something in between, our charge is to make an investment in you. We only have the right to our portion of your time if it's organized in a way to be of maximum benefit to you, as well as to us. No one can be great at everything. But if you aspire to be great in what matters most to you, I aspire to be at least competent in organizing our time together. If my goal is to be thought of as a teacher who helps develop good people as well as good players, the foundations of our program, the pillars we build everything on, should be organization, hard work, competition, and the personal development that results from your participation.

In the world we live in today, it's easier to be adaptable. Like many people my age and older, I may be uneasy with technology, but like it or not, the information revolution has irrevocably changed all our lives. We'd know a lot more about the past if we'd had such tools sooner. With the capability of such instant communications, no one is out of reach anymore. Whether you're running a business, heading a family, or coaching a team, carefully think out what you want to communicate with everyone who reports to you, and then add his or her input into the mix. Being organized is the only way to justify asking for the investment of anyone's time. It's not a right. It's a responsibility.

8. The eyes speak for the heart.

We hear a lot about multi-tasking these days, the ability to do many things in the same time frame. In midwinter we are advised to consider multi-layering, to go out more fully protected against the wind and chill. In coaching, whatever your own setting, I think it is more like a kind of multi-sensoring. Sometimes we need to speak and to see, to look and listen, at the same time. Like most skills, it can only be acquired through experience.

It was around 6:30 on the evening of Tuesday, November 14, 2006. We were about to play our first regular-season game, at home against the Fairfield University Stags. They had not beaten Saint Joseph's since 1978, but prior history means little in competitive sports. It is a short walk from my cluttered closet of an office across the court to what is probably also the smallest locker room in Division I basketball (though the visitors' room may be marginally smaller). However, such intimacy has its advantages. I can look directly into the eyes of every player, and he into mine.

I had my serious game face on. Our season really started in August as our players arrived with their fellow students for the new semester. During individual early-morning workouts, we coaches tried to gauge each player's potential. That was more challenging than in most previous seasons, because five of our fourteen players were freshmen, probably requiring a lot of individual attention. Thank heaven for the skills and sensitivity of my assistant coaches. The organized team practices begin in October, during which so many difficult decisions have to be made. Who will start? What returning players seem to have improved the most? What should our rotation be? Time, as always, is short.

As the exhibition games emerge and the non-conference schedule looms, everything seems to speed up. Being involved with the A-10 and Big 5, our overall schedule allows room for relatively few additional games, but we like to test ourselves early against the best. That season's opponents included Bucknell, Penn State, and potentially Louisville and St. John's at the NABC Classic and Holiday Festival tournaments. All before January.

You may recall "September Song" from an old Broadway show called *Knickerbocker Holiday*. "But it's a long, long while from May to December, and the days grow short when you reach September." With us it seems a very short time between November and March. Like every other team, we start even. But we're already looking forward to that secular Christmas at the end of the road in March called "Selection Sunday."

For only 65 of the 336 teams in Division I men's basketball, the coveted gift is a seeding, to be determined by conference championships and a committee of our peers, and predicted with his customary precision by that most brilliant and ubiquitous of bracketologists, Joe Lunardi. Let the office pools be distributed and the upsets begin. Like it or not, that's made the colossus of "March Madness" what it is.

We were not engaged in wagering, however, just planning, hoping, projecting, and probably praying. On that November night, the talent might have been in this room, but much of it was untested. We could hear that resounding St. Joe's drum outside keeping time with our beating hearts.

Standing in the center, with just enough room to stride back and forth a bit, I looked at each of my players, seated in a semicircle about me, and said the things I'd thought about telling them: "You've been prepared harder than any team I've had. You're prepared to perform, and you're performing for each other—so let's be prepared to perform to perfection. We've had our best two practices the last two days."

We'd already gone over specifics in terms of the opposing team, player by player. Then specifics to each of our starters: "Pat, you can't spin. You have to stay solid . . . . You all know the plan. You should know what your teammates can do. Trust the plan. Execute the plan . . . . You know what to do if they go to zone. On offense they will be in your chest. Set screens. Put your body on someone. Remember ball pressure. On defense, dominate the glass. You young players, apply what you've learned. Don't be brain-dead out there. When you shoot, it's not to take it, it's to make it. If we dominate, if we execute, if we sprint, they won't get to 50." (As it turned out, the final score was in our favor, 63 to 47.)

"We have only some thirty chances this season to do this," I concluded. "If you know the plan, and execute it, we'll win." The priest gave his blessing, and then we recited together the Lord's Prayer. Next, hands up and clasped together, "Saint Joseph, pray for us. Hawks on three . . . Shirts tucked in . . . Let's go!" Everyone rushed out the few feet to the court, and the crowd erupted. Could it really be only 3,200? Everyone went except me. I sat by myself for a moment, my head in my hands, before taking to the court about a minute and a half before the tip-off. The band was almost finished with "Oh When the Hawks Go Flying In!"

It wasn't because I longed to hear my name chanted by the student section, although I do appreciate that, and I shook my fist in acknowledgment. Once on the court, I shook hands with the opposing coach and the officials. It was just what I've always done, a combination of reflection and ritual. Similarly, when earlier I had come alone to the locker room, the players and other coaches were already assembled there.

I stressed to each player that his eyes have to be wide open throughout the game, adding, "Even if you're on the bench you have to be *in* the game." Throughout my pregame talk, I tried to take my own advice. I wasn't really listening to what I was saying. Call it multi-tasking or multi-sensoring—it's possible to really believe in what you're saying, to have thought it through without actually memorizing it, and then to talk and yet not to listen to yourself. Instead, I was scoping the room, looking into each player's eyes. What did they tell me? Did they show trust? Which player was fearful? Who was looking forward confidently to the contest? Who was distracted? Who was focused? What would happen during the next two hours had little to do with what I was saying.

The technical part of coaching is only the start. If I do have one specific imperative to the way I coach, it's to watch people's eyes. Are they cloudy or confident? Every person we meet has a different story going on, and their eyes express that story. To treat everyone fairly is not to treat them all the same. That player whose eyes show fear has to be motivated differently than the one whose eyes tell me he's fearless.

When did I know that the 2003–04 season would be special, one to be cherished forever? When I looked into the eyes of every player who took the time to comfort Dwayne Lee at his mother's funeral, who reached out their hands to touch his heart. For once, every pair of eyes revealed the same sentiments. There was no separation, whether of age or color or background or personality. I could only see similarity, a common compassion for a teammate that transcended each player's individuality. That recognition of a single set of eyes told me all I needed to know about the coming season.

Such direct knowledge can be adapted to teamwork in any field. In making all the technological advances we're so proud of, we've lost so much of what is real, what can only be learned through listening to a live voice, and looking directly into a pair of expressive eyes. All the "menus" of our machines are no substitute for the authentic customer service of a living, friendly face. The outstanding people in every field are skilled communicators, whatever their techniques, but to get your point across, you have to see who you're talking to, and how they react. Their eyes speak for their hearts.

9. In all that you do, work (and play) hard, smart, and together.

Sometimes, in whatever we do, it's hard to come up with just the right combination of words to send our sentiments soaring. I suppose that's why we have Hallmark. I was looking for a theme to help inspire my first team here at Saint Joseph's. What did I want them to do? Well, obviously, to win. To win consistently, they would have to play together. I think I read somewhere that the success of the team assures the success of the individual. But every other team comes in with that same mindset. Simply wanting to win doesn't separate you, in life or in sports, from your competition. Our team would also have to play smart—and, of course, they would have to play hard.

But that's almost a cliché. Saying after a game that our team played "hard" generally means that, despite all their efforts, we lost. Yes, failure is never fatal, and there are lessons in losing as well as in victory—but, put simply, I hadn't been hired to lose. Most of all, every successful team has to learn to play together. The first team I coached on Hawk Hill, whether because of or in spite of my efforts, won nineteen games, including four in the postseason NIT, before falling to Nebraska by four points. Our second team, in 1996–97, improved, winning twenty-six games, including two in the NCAA tournament's West Regional. It can't have been words alone that inspired them, but I do think that unwieldy combination of words that expressed our goals then and now—to work hard, smart, and together—does kind of sum up what we want to do. It's easier to be glib in print than in real life.

But what about those other words—to "play" hard, smart, and together? How a team works together translates into how they play. And by playing, I don't only mean in the actual games. I've mentioned that many of our players have viewed their overall college experience as enjoyable. When Jameer Nelson went into the pros, he said, "I just hope the NBA is this much fun." Does that extend to all his hours of intensive practice?

In his most frequently quoted comments, Allen Iverson, an NBA veteran justifiably celebrated for "playing every game like it's my last," questioned his coach's criticism of his relative indifference to practice schedules. "We're talking about *practice*," Iverson kept saying, "not the game." You see this interview on TV all the time. I'm never likely to coach in the pros, and I'd never criticize the work ethic of an Iverson, but I know that in the college game, performance in practice, more often than not, does translate into performance in game situations.

There's a difference between "fun" and "funny." Practices are meant to be competitive. If at the end of two and a half hours players feel they've had an enjoyable, even if exhausting, experience, that's what I mean by fun. They may even want to keep shooting for a while on their own. When that spirited reserve player who used to be on the Philadelphia Phillies shoved a cream pie into the face of every "star of the game" who was being interviewed on television, I'm sure he thought it was funny. Most of them seemed to take it well. However, putting shaving cream on a doorknob, for example, isn't any funnier than the destructive practice of just taking the knob off and tossing it. Young people should learn the difference.

Nothing was more fun for me as a kid than playing ball with all those guys I'd meet in other neighborhoods. Learning was fun. Practice was fun. All the activity and competition were fun. Some of what we did and said may also have been funny. Fortunately, life is full of funny situations, but they are incidents, not the focus of what we're doing.

As a coach today, I try to make certain that our practices are not excessively repetitive or monotonous. I want everyone to be totally engaged. And the instruction they receive is not all in one dominating voice. Some of it is player to player. Young people always want to measure themselves against others, whether it be in math or socially or athletically. If you measure yourself against the best, and against what you project yourself to be, that's the kind of challenge that can also constitute fun.

A thousand guys are going to try to sell cars today. You may be one of them. Why not set yourself apart? If you reach out, if you network through satisfied customers to gain new ones, if you've studied your product line thoroughly enough to explain how it exceeds your competitor's, if you're perpetually positive, if you work hard, if you work smart, and work smoothly together with your entire sales and service team, more often than not you and your dealership will come out on top. Just wanting to win won't do it. The *will* to win involves self-sacrifice. It takes time to learn all you need to know, to start early and work late. But there's no greater satisfaction than in the knowledge that you've done your best by mastering those three interrelated essential qualities: working and playing hard, smart, and together.

10. Never let others know if you are working or playing; make it seem that you are doing both at the same time.

Am I suggesting deception? Well, not exactly. Orison Marden, the founder of *Success* magazine, shares this thought with us: "A master in the art of living draws no sharp distinction between his work and his play, his mind and his body, his labor and his leisure, his education and his recreation. He hardly knows which is which." He simply pursues his own vision of excellence and leaves it to others to decide if he is working or playing. To himself he always seems to be doing both.

If you're not passionate about what you do, find something else. I'm no paragon. This past season, my twelfth at the helm at Saint Joseph's, where I've always stressed high standards and self-control to my players, I'm embarrassed to admit that I was reprimanded by the Atlantic 10 Conference. I'd made some negative comments about officiating after a tough loss to Penn State. I won't lie, but I did apologize. "My belief remains the same," I said. "There was a foul at the end of the game . . . [but] my efforts to express it were incorrect and embarrassing to my family and to my program."

I talked to the conference commissioner, the referee who was involved, and the coach of the other team, admitting that my conduct was "something I can't repeat." But chastened as we all are sometimes in life, I came back with no less passion for the next game, and the next. I've never viewed going to work as a job, and whatever you do, neither should you.

I believe that whether you're a parent, a coach, a teacher, a CEO, an office manager, a professional, or several of the above, you want the people who represent you to handle themselves in a certain way. Think of yourself as, say, a bartender, a bartender for life. Your success every night depends not only on your skill in mixing drinks but on your ability to listen, to communicate, to empathize, to sense how a person feels, to perceive a situation or a scenario. Quite a set of "people skills" are involved. Aren't they similar to the skills we expect all our coaches, our teachers, and our managers to master? If you're as attentive to body language and your surroundings as a skilled bartender has to be, you are bound to relate better to everyone around you.

However, I believe that if people working with you or representing you don't aspire to improve in this way, they are holding you back, as well as themselves. Whether their career objectives are wrapped up in titles or status or salary, I think you need to take a step back and consider, well, why did they come here in the first place? Are we just functioning as a location for them to spend time? Spending time really means killing time, yours and theirs. Sensitivity to others is essential in helping each of us pursue our own vision of excellence.

Passion belongs in the boardroom as well as in the bedroom, and in every workplace—if that's what we choose to call it. When I get up in the morning, I'm not preparing to go to work. I don't think Clare Ariano is either, or Don DiJulia, or a host of other people I'm likely to see that day. I'm not going to a job. I'm going to pursue my passion. If by the end of the day, whatever its challenges, things seem even a bit better, it's been a successful day. Even if we lose our game that night, tough and lingering as it can be, the disappointment doesn't diminish hope. When I have to be away, I'm not "missing work." Wherever I am, there's no separation between my work and my play, although I invest a lot of time in both.

So am I stealing money? In a way, but who's to say what someone's worth? The people at the top of my profession make an immense amount of money and have amazing perks, but the pressure to win is relentless. A great actor or musician makes millions, but the majority of others in their tenuous professions, who may be similarly or even more talented, just scrape by or are unemployed. Those, unfortunately, are the breaks in most creative endeavors. A researcher at an immense university may bring in contracts worth tens of millions, but is he more valuable than a great teacher? So long as we affirm the free enterprise system, this will always be a source of contention. We all wish life were more equitable, but success can't be guaranteed—only the opportunity to succeed, our own individual "pursuit of happiness."

What I do know is that I earn more than I ever imagined anyone could for doing something he loves. Yet, particularly after 2004, when I became a "hot" property (I'll define that later; I've talked enough about passion), I was offered coaching jobs at major universities at three or four times what it's remotely possible, generous though they are, for Saint Joseph's to pay me. As you probably know, at some public universities, the head football or basketball coach is by far the best-paid employee of the state. I'm no more averse to temptation than anyone else, but I'll never forget what Judy said to me after one of those offers, "So what's a couple hundred thousand less a year?" We still laugh about it, when I'm not crying.

You have to know where your heart is. I don't want to be on a pedestal, bigger than life, or in what amounts to a bubble, isolated from others. When you've got to be more, you can wind up being a lot less. There are many kinds of compensation. So I guess I'll remain where my heart resides, hopefully still the same regular guy trying to do better, surrounded by people who share the same passion. With apologies to Kermit the Frog, it's not easy turning down green, but I'm not planning to go anywhere.

In the real world we all inhabit, if your company, your school, your family, or even your bar is a happier place because of something you did today, you're in the right place. If the team you're on was better today because of your work and play, you've had a great day. Which is what I want for everyone who has been good enough to read this book.

CHAPTER 10

Keep the Hawk Aloft!

To everything there is a season. There may be no win-
dows in my cozy closet of an office, but I know the leaves are
falling outside. It's brisk everywhere around Hawk Hill these
days. Hopes are high, and hearts beat harder than usual. Another
basketball season is about to start, officially that of 2007–08. Of
course, it is only one component, and not nearly the most important, in the composite calendar that brings our whole campus back to bustling life every fall. It is, however, the component
for which my staff and I are responsible. Through our efforts, we
strive for excellence in the same way as those departments
charged with teaching English, philosophy, or business.

What defines excellence? I don't have my *Bartlett's* handy, but
I recall that sage who wished for future generations that they live
in "interesting" times. That's the least of our problems today. We
may never see another placid decade. It's odd. Throughout history those periods of greatest creativity seem to have come

during the most turbulent of times. While hardly equating excellence in basketball with the Renaissance, Bill Walton recently
recalled that only the sustained success of its basketball program united virtually everyone around UCLA during the turmoil
of the 1960s and '70s. Pauley Pavilion became his own personal
place of refuge, and when his team was playing its best it was
like a joyous, shared "celebration of life." Sports can have that
power, whether it really makes sense or not.

Eighteen wins hardly constitute a debacle, but our own team
was surely not at its best throughout last season's fluctuating
fortunes. For the first time in seven years, we didn't get to the
postseason. I'm happy to say that our women's team, under the
dynamic Cindy Griffin, did advance to their WNIT, and that at
least one Martelli, my son, Phil Jr., did make it into the "Big
Dance," at least briefly, as an assistant to that great Philly guy,
Joe Mihalich, at Niagara. In just about everything off-court our
own team was exceptional—in its work attitude, in its commitment to charitable activities, and in being responsible student-
athletes. But for whatever reasons, that attitude simply didn't
translate into consistent success *on* the court.

It's true that our normal rotation included four freshmen. As
the late Al McGuire used to say, the best thing about freshmen
is that they become sophomores. A year stronger and smarter,
buoyed by the talents of our seniors and juniors, we harbor
greater expectations for this coming season. Don't give up on
us yet. Whatever happens, the ultimate responsibility comes
back to me. Through that constant hum of activity around here
that everyone's so used to, I've lately been hearing the strains
of an old song from *Kiss Me Kate:* "Another op'nin', another
show, in Philly, Boston, or Baltimo . . . another pain where the
ulcers grow . . . ."

Even if we're not about to get ulcers, we should have all
learned a lot through our shared season of disappointment. We

have to do everything better. We coaches have to motivate better, and those we coach have to play better together. Despite all the mega-hyped excesses of the media, I still view college sports as more an exercise in education than entertainment. There is an undeniable joy in performing your best, in getting better with each game. For our legion of fans, that can certainly be entertaining. A great game *is* a great show. Yet there's more than one measure of success. Let's try to keep it in perspective. Winning is great, but it's more important to become a winner. Wasn't it that renowned Philly guy Ben Franklin who originated the concept of the student-athlete?

I trust that this book has been more than a chronicle of seasons. It's my conversation with you, an extension of my ongoing conversation with all those around me each day. But communication is a two-way street. I hope to hear a lot of what *you* have to say as I go around the country voicing the messages these pages contain—that we are all in the business of people, that we are all coaches, that we each have within us our own unique book, that the ability to listen underlies the commitment to learn. Each of us evolves as everything around us changes. We should challenge each other to do better, to be more open, to listen and learn, to articulate our feelings thoughtfully and honestly, and—most of all—to work *with* others rather than hiding behind the façade of whatever title we've been labeled with.

Such an emphasis is becoming more difficult all the time, as the pace of everyone's life is speeded up by relentless technology. To my parents, the art of carefully crafted letter writing is still a reality. To my children, communication is hastened by the impersonal speed of text messages, saying as little of substance as possible. How often do we still see people face-to-face? How often do we really listen? How often do we put pen to paper and take the time to think through what we want to say? I can see, feel, and taste everything I've wanted to include in this book, but I still have more questions than answers. Maybe you can provide some. Just as conversation is a two-way street, motivation comes from more than one direction.

As with individuals, teams can develop distinct personalities. The overall attentiveness of our current team, despite its low-key demeanor last season, encourages my assistant coaches and me to believe in their potential to perform more consistently, a necessary quality to success in every walk of life. I like to think that, as with my children, I've had no favorite team. Of course, the achievements of the 2003–04 group were special, but I've enjoyed working with every team I've coached.

I have no unique insight, but I do get to see a lot of young people at that crucial juncture between high school and college. In many ways, our high-profile athletes, college or professional, can be viewed as a reflection of where we are as a society, and where we seem to be going. If I were to focus only on this slender segment of our youth, I'd be less sanguine about the future. Anyone involved in recruiting coveted high-school athletes today will testify to how many tend to see the world solely through the pinhole of their own identity. They've been conditioned to think of themselves first and foremost. If they're skilled enough, they seem convinced that they can get away with almost anything. They know others are committed to cash in on their skills.

We do a lot of recruiting, but I've enjoyed the great advantage at this university of focusing on young people whose talents appear to be matched by their character. Over the years I've certainly made mistakes, but I think we've been disappointed far more frequently by the performances of players on the court than by their misbehavior off it. As a practical matter, we have to recruit exceptional talent to compete in Division I basketball, but experience continues to demonstrate that character is more important than talent alone. To be "coachable" implies the capacity to listen and learn, to keep getting better.

Speaking of conversations and communications, because I've written so much about the people who make things go in my world, I thought I should solicit some return input. The trouble with Clare Ariano is that she never says anything negative about anybody. Still, we asked her what she's liked and disliked most about working with me these past twenty years. Much of it sounds like she's describing jolly old Saint Nick: "Phil's always ready with a quick quip, a smile to match, and a twinkle in his eyes. Whether in the office or on *HawkTalk*, he does his best to lighten the stressful atmosphere of coaching a competitive sports team." I loved reading about how I'm always giving back, how I'm appreciative of everyone's efforts, how I'm devoted to my family, and how my "crinkled eyes" (am I still in my fifties?) are never closed to anyone with a problem or a concern. Didn't I tell you?

We finally eked out of her that I'm constantly yelling from my cluttered old locker-room of an office, "Clare!" "Mark!" "Doug!" "David!" "Sully!" I guess that's better than Dancer, Prancer, Donder, Blitzen, and Rudolph. And she did mention such occasions as during basketball camp when, hearing her name chanted louder and louder, she had to come onto the adjacent court and make a foul shot. Talk about pressure. She said $100 was riding on it, but would I take money from a kid? Remember, I said I wasn't about to steal anyone's time or money.

And speaking of both Clare and *HawkTalk*, our guests were more varied and informative than ever in our eleventh season—from thoughtful Jon Runyan of the Philadelphia Eagles to former Phillie Mitch "Wild Thing" Williams. Our crack research staff had discovered that Mitch managed Atlantic City's professional baseball team, which was especially relevant because the Atlantic 10 tournament would be held for the first time in Atlantic City's Boardwalk Hall. It turned out that Williams hadn't managed the Surf for two and a half years, but he handled it tactfully and was an engaging guest. Despite that Joe Carter home run, Mitch will always be remembered fondly by Phillies fans, and in fact is now doing some broadcasting. "Yes, I can still throw," he said. "I just can't stand up."

Many people think *HawkTalk* is on throughout the season because it's so memorable, but that might be too exhausting for everyone involved. The fact is, last year we had only eight shows on television, and nine on radio. As always, we worked in a lot about Saint Joseph's, past and present—from the return of John Smith, who made so many memorable shots a quarter-century ago, to hearing about the three hundred current students who spent *their* spring break not in Cancun but immersed in an "Appalachian Experience," helping out the residents of one of America's most impoverished regions. This kind of commitment by so many of our young people, here as elsewhere, should be more publicized, as opposed to the excessive focus on a relative handful of self-centered "high flyers" and "diaper dandies."

On *HawkTalk* early in February, we announced that this book would be coming out in the fall. My top ten list was of *other* titles we'd considered for the book. They encompassed both the season we were having and popular TV shows. Some didn't have to be changed, such as *Lost* and *Curb Your Enthusiasm* (or was it "Curb Your Turnovers"?). Others were modestly revised: *Phil and Grace*; *Joe's Anatomy*; *Desperate Game Plans*; *Steal or No Steal*; *CSI-Hawk Hill*; *Boston Illegal Screens*; *Prison Break—or the St. Joe's Transition Game*.

I admitted to hearing voices, with my Jekyll and Hyde team combining as many identities as Sybil. We just hoped to sustain some semblance of our sanity. "Clare Voyant" was as accurate as usual, although *HawkTalk* didn't win a deserved Golden Globe for the eleventh consecutive year. She did have one modest lapse, however, in loyally predicting for us a national championship in 2007. Wrong year. Wisconsin was her "dark horse." I hope Bo Ryan appreciates that.

As usual, Joe Lunardi and I got to talk more on the radio show about each of the games, fielding the questions of our many stubbornly supportive callers. I suggested that Xavier reminded me of Noah's ark, with two of everything, and that yes, the Richmond coach volunteered that his team had played their best game of the season in beating us. Not much solace there. Well, it's not easy. I don't think I'll ever be defined as a gracious loser. The will to win is too deeply embedded in my DNA. Wait a minute. Didn't I say something about keeping it all in perspective? Basketball is really a two-dimensional game, from the neck up and the neck down.

When Joe departed for his annual bracketology tour, making more appearances than a presidential candidate, he generously suggested that at least I'd asked all the right questions of our team in 2006–07. Maybe we'll get more of the right answers in 2007–08. Whatever happens, we can hardly wait.

As usual, our final *HawkTalk* on television last season was the most memorable. We had only one graduating senior from the team, our "man for all seasons," the towering Artur Surov, an honor student in management, as well as our head manager, the genial Dan Timby. Our most debonair assistant coach of all time returned—Monté Ross, who's now head coach at Delaware. As with our own team last season, he'd had "a tough year, but a wonderful experience." Just like me, he "slept like a baby," which meant waking up every two hours, crying. Oddly, he'd never been on *HawkTalk* before, and as a guest was obliged to keep the distinctive T-shirt we've started giving out, whether he wanted to or not. It was great seeing him.

It's funny, we now have three executive producers on *Hawk-Talk*, yet I can't find one legitimate seven-footer for our team. Well, we're headed for "another season we hope will last, to make your future forget your past." Don't you love those old Broadway shows?

Waxing nostalgic, after thanking Britney Spears for copying my hairstyle, I'd compiled a top ten list of special dates in my life. Here they are:

> ► December 1975—I propose to Judy. She holds out for a ring, disdaining the one in the Cracker Jack box.

> ► September 1985—I come to Hawk Hill as an assistant coach, finding the Fieldhouse by only my second day on the job.

> ► September 1999—Phil Martelli Jr. becomes a freshman at St. Joe's—the first recruit I got by sleeping with his mother. (That's as risqué as we get, but this *is* cable television.)

> ► February 2001—*HawkTalk* is named best coach's show on television by *The Sporting News*. Nielsen reports that our audience rises to double digits.

> ► March 2004—We're a number-one seed. No joke.

> ► April 2004—I'm named National Coach of the Year, the best honor money can buy.

> ► May 2004—I make the commencement address at Widener. No one walks out.

> ► May 2005—I throw out the first pitch at a Phillies game. Mike Lieberthal misses it, but Pat Burrell takes it for a called third strike.

▶ May 2006—Only two years after Widener, I speak at Cabrini. I'm on a roll—*Dr.* Martelli.

▶ Culminating in 2007—Our team wins its 50th, 100th, and 200th games under my tenure as head coach, all against St. Bonaventure. No honorary degree there.

Now, SINCE IT's time to look ahead, here are ten things I'd like to see this coming season:

❶ All St. Joe's games will be sold out—home, away, and at neutral sites.

❷ The FCC informs smiling Joe Lunardi that his bracketology can be exhibited on no more than three networks at the same time, with a five-minute limit on close-ups.

❸ Jay Wright of Villanova has to shave his head on *his* coach's show to give us some visual parity.

❹ The Big 5 has a banner year, with multiple teams in the postseason.

❺ Artur Surov replaces Craig LaBan as the *Inquirer*'s food critic, then goes on to win "Wing Bowl."

❻ The A-10 tournament remains in Atlantic City, but our communications director, Marie Wozniak, has to return when it's over.

❼ Every Big 5 game will be played in the Palestra, with the NCAA providing streamers for *all* the games.

❽ *Don't Call Me Coach* is adapted to a motion

picture titled *Inexplicable*, with Mark Walhberg in the lead role.

9 Fran Dunphy shares his secret of how to become the most likeable coach in America.

10 The NCAA selection committee decides to broadcast its proceedings live on national television, guaranteeing higher ratings than even the final episode of *The Sopranos*.

How far we go in this life isn't measured in miles. It is not all that far from where I grew up or where I live now to Hawk Hill. Yet what I do here has taken me all around the world. Prior to one season, I took my squad on a tour of Italy, playing local teams and experiencing wonderful sights. I look forward to doing it again. In the summer of 2005, I served as head coach of the USA Men's Under 21 World Championship team, which played in Argentina. I was assistant coach for our gold-medal-winning teams at both the 2001 FIBA World Championships for Young Men, in Japan, and the 1998 Goodwill Games.

No one has benefited more than I have from what Jack McKinney in a memorable speech defined as "the brotherhood of basketball." Of course it's now a sisterhood, as well. Yes, it is only a game, not a religion. But for me it has always held a special allure. As John Feinstein once wrote, "I love baseball . . . . But I *live* basketball, specifically college basketball."

Whatever *you* choose to do, why not aim high and blaze new trails? As Barbara Bush said at the 1990 Wellesley Commencement, "Who knows? Somewhere out in this audience may even be someone who one day will follow in my footsteps and preside over the White House as the President's spouse . . . and I wish *him* well."

I hope that each of you, my companions in this conversation of shared experiences, may also have benefited in some modest measure from these reflections. And I look forward to seeing and hearing from you along the way. We may come and go, but the Hawk never dies. Or, as my collaborator in this book prefers to put it, "The Hawk remains eternally aloft!" As I said on page one, the qualities it represents are special to me in so many ways. "The Hawk Will Never Die!" is not simply a slogan, limited in its significance to those of us who are related to this specific university. It embodies a way of living, and the will to never give up. That message is something we can *all* share. Thanks for listening.